'This adventurous, compassionate book wakes us up to the experience of limerence. With myths, real-life cases, and timely insight into digital limerence, Orly Miller offers practical guidance for both clinicians and individuals, and beautifully shows that healing is possible.'

Lucy L. Brown, PhD, *Neuroscientist, Albert Einstein College of Medicine*

'Orly Miller offers a fresh new perspective on the commonly occurring but often misunderstood experience of limerence. Her work is both incisive and holistic, making it a powerful read for therapists and laypeople alike. If you are looking for an analytic deep dive into the world of intense longing, this book is for you.'

Alexandra H. Solomon, PhD, *Adjunct Professor at Northwestern University, bestselling author of* Love Every Day, *and Host of the Podcast*, Reimagining Love

Limerence

What happens when longing takes hold and won't let go? When the need for connection becomes obsession, and fantasy begins to blur with reality?

This book explores limerence, a complex and often misunderstood psychological state marked by intrusive thoughts, emotional dependency, and an intense longing for reciprocation. What begins as attraction can quickly spiral into fixation, projection, and the gradual unravelling of the self.

The author weaves together insights from psychology, neuroscience, mythology, and cultural analysis to examine limerence through clinical, emotional, symbolic, digital, spiritual, and relational lenses. Drawing on case studies, archetypal patterns, and original diagnostic frameworks, it reveals limerence as both a source of profound suffering and a window into deeper psychological truths.

For therapists, clinicians, and curious readers alike, this is a nuanced exploration of obsessive love and the psychological complexities that shape it.

Orly Miller is a psychologist and writer whose work explores the terrain of obsessive love, emotional attachment, and longing. Drawing on clinical practice, mythology, and cultural critique, she brings a unique lens to limerence, blending therapeutic insight with literary and symbolic analysis.

Limerence
The Psychopathology of Loving Too Much

Orly Miller

Routledge
Taylor & Francis Group

LONDON AND NEW YORK

Designed cover image: duncan1890

First published 2026
by Routledge
4 Park Square, Milton Park, Abingdon, Oxon OX14 4RN

and by Routledge
605 Third Avenue, New York, NY 10158

Routledge is an imprint of the Taylor & Francis Group, an informa business

© 2026 Orly Miller

For Product Safety Concerns and Information please contact our EU representative GPSR@taylorandfrancis.com. Taylor & Francis Verlag GmbH, Kaufingerstraße 24, 80331 München, Germany.

British Library Cataloguing-in-Publication Data
A catalogue record for this book is available from the British Library

ISBN: 9781032915326 (hbk)
ISBN: 9781032915319 (pbk)
ISBN: 9781003563747 (ebk)

DOI: 10.4324/9781003563747

Typeset in Galliard
by codeMantra

For my family.

Contents

Figures

Preface

There are kinds of love that nourish, and kinds that consume. This book is about the latter.

Limerence is a psychic fire. An ache that moves like obsession but disguises itself as devotion. It is a hunger, a haunting, a beautiful torment. It arrives without warning and resists all logic. You do not choose it. You are chosen.

I did not set out to write this book. It gathered slowly, like smoke rising through my clinical work, my conversations, my own reflections.

Over time, it became clear that this experience needed language and recognition. Because it hurts. Because it matters. Because it reveals something about the soul of longing.

This book is my offering. Burning, I place it on the altar of Love. For the psyche, for the soul, for the sanctity of human connection. Let it burn. Let something true be revealed.

Acknowledgments

This book did not come into being alone, though solitude played its part.

Thank you to Hugh Kingsley, Elli Tamir, Dr. Gil Korman, Cherie Levie, Dion Kagan, and Louise Merrington for your conversations, critical eyes, and for pointing me toward doors I did not know how to find, let alone open.

To Jaye Huxley, Helen Wolfers, Maya Lester, and David Michael, thank you for your support and presence.

To my mother, Debbie Masel. May her memory be a blessing. Thank you for the blueprint of the writing life and for appearing when invoked.

To my clients and to those who shared your stories of obsessive love, thank you for entrusting me with your secrets. All names and identifying details have been changed to preserve confidentiality, but the essence and insight remain.

Acronyms and Abbreviations

AI	artificial intelligence
BPD	borderline personality disorder
CBT	cognitive behavioral therapy
DBT	dialectical behavior therapy
DSM	diagnostic and statistical manual of mental disorders
DSM-5-TR	diagnostic and statistical manual of mental disorders, fifth edition, text revision
fMRI	functional magnetic resonance imaging
GAD	generalized anxiety disorder
LAS	limerence assessment scale
OCD	obsessive–compulsive disorder
OLD	obsessive love disorder
PET	positron emission tomography
RAIN	recognize, allow, investigate, and nurture
SAD	separation anxiety disorder

Introduction

Limerence in Context: A Passionate Madness

Limerence is an acute, disruptive, and enduring state of intense longing for a specific person that is characterized by intrusive and obsessive thoughts, fantasies, emotional volatility, and a powerful desire for emotional reciprocation. Limerence is not the same as a crush, nor is it part of healthy love. While limerence may resemble the early stages of a healthy love relationship, it is distinctly different. The distinction lies in what happens next. In a healthy love relationship, the initial infatuation period will give way to another phase. Either the couple will bond successfully and enter a tangible relationship, or they will not, perhaps grieve the romantic attachment, and move on, maintaining a platonic friendship or going their separate ways.

A crush typically involves attraction, curiosity, or admiration, but remains light and manageable. It does not take hold of the psyche in the same way as limerence, nor does it cause the same level of psychological disruption. If the feelings are unrequited or the circumstances are unfavorable, the person with a crush is generally able to accept this and let go. In this way, the trajectory of a crush is closer to that of healthy love: it either progresses or fades.

Limerence doesn't move beyond infatuation, but rather keeps the individual transfixed and obsessed by another, regardless of the relationship's viability or progress. Limerence thrives in uncertainty, flourishing when a person is unsure about their standing with the one they desire or when a barrier prevents the connection from developing into a real, reciprocal, and fulfilling relationship. It can be agonizing and last for months, years, or even decades, sustained by a potent mix of hope and doubt.

Limerence encompasses a wide spectrum of intense emotions, ranging from ecstatic highs to profound lows. On the darker side, it involves depressed moods, irritability, anxiety, low self-esteem, obsessive thoughts, and suicidal ideation. However, limerence is not all darkness and gloom. The highs can be euphoric, invoking feelings of love, connection, energy, heightened self-esteem, joy, enhanced sensory awareness, increased libido, and an experience of spiritual connection and bliss.

Due to the powerfully intense and volatile emotional landscape of limerence, it also serves as a powerful muse. It has imbued human expression with sensual and creative energy, fueling many great works of art, literature, music,

DOI: 10.4324/9781003563747-1

and film throughout the ages. The emotional intensity of limerence has also stoked the flames of many passionate relationships and affairs of the heart, both real and imagined, condoned and condemned.

While the direction of emotions fluctuates during limerence, the intensity remains constant. People experiencing limerence swing wildly between euphoria and depression, sometimes within a single day or night. The direction of the intense emotions depends on the perceived level of emotional reciprocation or rejection from the desired other, determined by interactions, both real and imagined.

Each interaction is imbued with so much meaning that it is replayed repeatedly, almost religiously, with every detail scrutinized for signs of reciprocation or rejection. The conclusions drawn from these interactions, however speculative, dictate the emotional direction the limerent individual experiences. This process, almost mystical, involves gleaning insight through symbols, subtle cues, choice of words, gestures, a change in breath, or a prolonged gaze. It is like interpreting a poem or deciphering a dream, grasping for glimmers of meaning and hope. It involves relentless self-torment, analyzing everything, and searching for invisible clues that might provide insight into the heart and mind of the other, resembling an intense and dangerous game of "she loves me, she loves me not."

This intense and prolonged obsession with another person severely disrupts important areas of life, impairing the individual's ability to work, focus, function, and maintain healthy relationships. The lack of awareness within the mental health community about limerence and its symptoms exacerbates its debilitating and isolating effects.

Given its psychological intensity and potential for harm, it is surprising that limerence has not been researched more extensively. Further investigation is needed to better understand limerence, including why it occurs in some individuals and not others, as well as the biological and environmental factors that contribute to its development and maintenance.

Since its initial conceptualization by psychologist Dorothy Tennov in the 1970s (Tennov, 1979), limerence has not received much research attention. Recently, however, it has reemerged in pop psychology as a topic of discussion on online forums and social media platforms. Articles in a range of media have featured limerence, attempting, and often failing, to clear up misconceptions and define what it actually is.

One has only to type the word "limerence" into a Google search to be confronted with questions like: "What is the difference between limerence and love?," "What are the signs and stages of limerence?," "Is limerence a sign of mental health issues?," "How is limerence treated?," "What are the causes and symptoms of limerence?," and "How can I overcome limerence?." While little is currently known about limerence, it is clear that many people are seeking information and support for it.

Limerence is not recognized as a psychological disorder in the current (fifth) edition of the *Diagnostic and Statistical Manual of Mental Disorders*

(DSM). Some mental health professionals use this to argue that limerence is therefore not pathological, but this reasoning is flawed. The DSM is a living document that undergoes continuous revisions as societal and cultural understandings evolve, and as new insights emerge regarding the psyche, personality, and behavior.

For example, in the first edition of the DSM, published in 1952, homosexuality was classified as a mental disorder (American Psychiatric Association [APA], 1952). It was removed in 1973 following a decision by the American Psychiatric Association, leading to new understandings of homosexuality and LGBTQIA+ identities (APA, 1980; Drescher, 2015). Generalized anxiety disorder (GAD) was not included in the DSM until the third edition in 1980 (APA, 1980). Similarly, borderline personality disorder (BPD), now a well-established diagnosis, was once dismissed and misunderstood. It was often regarded as a collection of difficult traits rather than a coherent clinical syndrome. Through the work of psychologist Marsha Linehan, who developed dialectical behavior therapy (DBT) as a targeted treatment, BPD began to be taken seriously, and it was added to the third edition of the DSM in 1980 (APA, 1980; Linehan, 1993).

Limerence may find its way into a future edition of the DSM if researchers start to pay it more attention. Limerence is a prolonged, intrusive state marked by disturbances in cognition, emotional regulation, and behavior, and is highly disruptive to normal functioning. More research is needed to understand limerence, categorize its symptoms, and identify its patterns of distress. With increased awareness, people suffering from limerence may have a better chance of understanding their experience, receiving adequate treatment, and embarking on a journey toward healing and recovery.

Many psychologists and psychiatrists haven't heard of limerence. Among those who are aware of it, there are differing perspectives. Limerence is sometimes presented as synonymous with the early stage of a normal love relationship; however, recent discourse and emerging research suggest otherwise.

US-based psychology academics Wakin and Vo (2008) propose a pathological model of limerence, distinguishing it from normative love and emphasizing its obsessive–compulsive and addictive features. They describe limerence as an involuntary, "negative, problematic, and impairing" condition with potential clinical significance, drawing structured parallels to substance dependence and obsessive–compulsive disorder (Wakin & Vo, 2008, p. 2). Similarly, UK-based researchers Willmott and Bentley (2015) identify links between limerence and psychological issues such as anxiety, depression, addiction, and trauma-related symptoms, emphasizing its obsessive qualities and potential for pathology, and calling for greater awareness and further research.

Forensic psychology and criminology scholars Bradbury, Short, and Bleakley (2024) conceptualize limerence as a consuming cognitive state marked by obsessive rumination, emotional intensity, and fixation, with parallels to obsessive–compulsive and delusional disorders, while US-based researcher and psychotherapist Wyant (2021) proposes a clinical conceptualization of limerence as a condition resembling obsessive–compulsive disorder, marked by intrusive thoughts, compulsive rituals, and emotional dependency.

In her original work on limerence, Tennov suggested that limerence may be a natural psychological mechanism for fostering romantic attachment and pair bonding. She also acknowledged that her work was a "preliminary report that only scratches the surface" of limerence and advocated for further research (Tennov, 1979, p. xi).

Core emotional states exist on a spectrum and may become pathological when they manifest with excessive intensity, persistence, and impairment. Sadness, for example, is a normal emotion, but when persistent and accompanied by cognitive and physical symptoms, it can indicate major depressive disorder. Anxiety, when chronic, pervasive, and difficult to control, may meet the criteria for GAD. Fear, when irrational and overwhelming, can present as specific phobias. Disgust, particularly when directed toward one's own body, may contribute to body dysmorphic disorder. In a similar way, love and desire, when experienced as obsessive, intrusive, and distressing, may become limerence.

Whether limerence is recognized as a unique mental health disorder will be determined by further research, but it is clear that limerence has undeniably pathological elements. Due to the lack of awareness about limerence in the mental health community, people experiencing it often suffer alone and in the dark. Numerous clients have approached me specifically seeking help with their experience of limerence. Time and again, I hear the same story: they went to a therapist to seek help for limerence and were met with a lack of understanding and insufficient support.

Well-meaning but misguided therapists advise these clients to "focus on something else" or to "just let go of the story." While this may be well-intended advice, it certainly isn't helpful. Just as people suffering from anxiety, depression, or obsessive–compulsive disorder can't simply "stop thinking about it," people experiencing limerence can't just "let go of the story and move on." If they could, believe me, they would.

Emotions

Love, along with other emotions, has long been considered separate from rational thought in philosophical and psychological discourse. Plato described emotions as wild horses that need to be reined in by intellect (Plato, 1911), while Descartes described passion as a disturbance of the soul (Clarke, 2003). When we are overtaken by strong emotions like anger or love, we arguably lose control of rational thought. The question is posed: If emotions aren't based on rational thought, what exactly are they? The answer is: we don't know. It seems that defining emotions is quite challenging (Fehr & Russell, 1984).

Throughout history, focus on emotions in psychological and philosophical discourse has fluctuated. Descartes proposed that the study of consciousness should be the primary focus in the realm of psychological discussion. His renowned statement, "I think, therefore I am," suggests that our conscious mind is what defines our functioning and existence (Descartes, 1996, Meditation II). Freud later challenged this philosophy by proposing that most of our mind is unconscious, and that our conscious knowledge about ourselves and the world represents only a fraction of the whole (Freud, 2002).

Freud proposed that emotional memories are kept in our unconscious mind, influencing our current emotions, thoughts, perceptions, and behaviors without our awareness (Freud, 2002). Later, behaviorists such as John B. Watson and B. F. Skinner rejected Freud's idea of the unconscious. They argued that psychology should focus solely on observable behaviors, neglecting what would later be referred to as the enigmatic "black box" of the hidden mind (Watson, 1929).

A significant shift occurred in the middle of the 20th century with the advent of computers. This sparked the proposal that the mind may operate similarly to a computer, giving rise to the emergence of the computer metaphors in cognitive psychology (Goldstein, 2004). Cognitive psychology, which views the mind as an information-processing tool, remains at the forefront of psychological discourse today. It reintroduced Freud's concept of the unconscious, but with a different perspective. Rather than focusing on the content of the unconscious, cognitive psychology examines the unconscious processes that generate conscious thought.

Cognitive psychology has greatly enriched our understanding of mental processes. However, it has largely overlooked one notable aspect: emotions (LeDoux, 1998). Cognitive psychology tends to place emotions in the too-hard basket, prioritizing cognitive processes over emotional experiences.

Understanding emotions is essential for a comprehensive understanding of the mind and human behavior. Emotions are not mere fleeting states; they are powerful forces that shape our thoughts, decisions, and actions (Lerner et al., 2015). They influence our perceptions of the world, enrich our experiences, and play a pivotal role in our relationships with others (Planalp et al., 2018). Emotions have a profound impact on our physical and psychological wellbeing and play a significant role in determining our overall life success (Goleman, 1996).

Insight into the evolutionary purpose of emotions and our understanding of the neurochemical aspects behind them offer some valuable knowledge, yet the fundamental essence and functions of these profound experiences continue to elude us. While we have made progress in unravelling the brain chemistry underlying certain emotions, the reasons why some emotions can become dysfunctional remain a mystery. We have yet to discover why admiration may transform into jealousy, desire into greed, or love into obsession (LeDoux, 1998).

Love

To understand limerence, we must first contemplate love. Love is a complex and multifaceted experience that has served as a wellspring of countless creations and artistic expressions throughout human history. From a spiritual perspective, love is perceived as a fundamental and transformative force that transcends the boundaries of the material realm (Azdajic, 2016). It is regarded as a gateway for humanity to experience and express divinity through connection with self and others.

From an evolutionary standpoint, love is recognized as an essential function that promotes the reproduction and survival of offspring (Fletcher et al., 2015). The love bond between partners plays a crucial role in successful mating, establishing stable partnerships, and ensuring the care and survival of future generations.

Each love relationship is unique, with its own story and journey. While cultural differences influence the formation and trajectory of relationships, love generally progresses through recognizable stages. The first stage in the love bond is usually infatuation, characterized by intense attraction, excitement, and a strong desire to be close to the person of interest. The infatuation stage involves passionate feelings and a strong focus on physical and sexual attraction.

The second stage is typically romantic love, which involves a deeper emotional connection, increased intimacy, and a sense of exclusivity. Passion and excitement continue to hold significance during this stage, but the focus shifts toward establishing a deeper and more exclusive connection.

The third and final stage of the successful love bond is attachment, where the relationship becomes more stable and long-term. If healthy, the attachment stage is marked by a sense of commitment, trust, and deep emotional union. Intimacy and companionship contribute to a relationship characterized by security and mutual support.

Though often mistaken for early romantic love, limerence follows a very different path, one marked by obsession, idealization, and suffering. Understanding this distinction is vital, both for those experiencing it and for those supporting them.

Limerence

The term "limerence" was coined by psychologist Dorothy Tennov in the 1970s. She introduced the word to describe a specific psychological state she observed in a subset of participants in her research on romantic love. Tennov described limerence as a state characterized by intrusive and obsessive thoughts, emotional fluctuations, longing, and a strong desire for emotional reciprocation (Tennov, 1979).

Interestingly, Tennov simply made up the word "limerence." It has no established etymology. In her own words: "I first used the term 'amorance,' then changed it back to 'limerence'... It has no roots whatsoever. It looks nice. It works well in French" (Observer, 1977).

Tennov initially proposed that limerence might be part of the infatuation phase in relationship formation, but she also observed that limerence is not present in every relationship and can also occur outside the context of romantic relationships. She advocated for further research to better understand limerence and to explore potential pathological elements and clinical implications (Tennov, 1979).

Limerence typically begins with intense attraction, accompanied by deep fascination, infatuation, and a strong desire for closeness with the desired person. As the attachment deepens, thoughts and fantasies about the desired person become more frequent and emotionally charged. Over time, these mental preoccupations become intrusive, obsessive, and difficult to control. Combined with intense longing and emotional volatility, limerence begins to disrupt daily functioning, affecting work, sleep, appetite, relationships, and overall wellbeing.

Initially, thoughts and fantasies about the desired person may feel pleasurable, as they trigger a surge of dopamine and other mood-enhancing neurochemicals. The limerent individual willingly sets aside time to be alone to think or fantasize about the desired person. This behavior quickly becomes addictive and difficult to control, intensifying the craving for more thoughts and fantasies, and thus perpetuating the cycle.

The fantasies surrounding the desired person intensify as the limerent individual continues to idealize them, attributing extraordinary and almost mythical qualities to them. Even their apparent flaws become desirable to the limerent individual, often to the bewilderment of those around them. The need for emotional reciprocation becomes overwhelmingly strong, driving the limerent individual to continuously seek affection, attention, and love from the desired other, either in reality or through fantasy.

During limerence's most intense phase, the limerent individual becomes completely consumed by an overwhelming obsession with the desired other, permeating every aspect of their thoughts, emotions, and inner life. This intense longing, yearning, persistent seeking of emotional reciprocation, fear of rejection, frequent obsessive and intrusive thoughts, and lack of support lead to significant suffering.

There is a common assumption in online articles that limerence only develops in situations of unrequited love or when there is the potential for a relationship to form. However, this is not the case. Limerence can arise at any time, in any situation, and with anyone. In some rare instances, it can even manifest as an imaginary relationship with someone the person has never met, such as a celebrity or social media influencer. The advent of technology and AI interfaces is introducing new risks for the development of obsessive attachments to digital entities.

More commonly, limerence develops in the context of someone known to the individual. One example is limerence sparked by a person encountered in daily life who is not well-known, such as a barista at a cafe, a regular passenger on a train commute, or a coworker observed from across the office. The initial attraction gives way to a flood of obsessive thoughts, fantasies, and longing, accompanied by a strong desire for emotional reciprocation.

Another scenario in which limerence can develop is within the context of a friendship or a potential sexual or romantic relationship. The limerent individual becomes consumed by the desire to obtain mutual affection and to develop a deeper romantic bond with the desired other. In this state, they may feel emotionally overwhelmed, isolated, and despairing. Their obsessive thoughts become a constant distraction, leading to problematic behaviors and impairing their ability to function effectively in daily life.

Limerence can affect anyone, regardless of their life circumstances or relationship status. A person does not need to be single or actively seeking a romantic connection to become limerent. Even those who are married or in committed relationships can find themselves caught in the grip of limerence for someone else. This experience can be confusing, isolating, and deeply distressing for both the individual and their partner, and it can have serious consequences for the relationship. Conflict, emotional withdrawal, neglect, and even marital breakdown may result from fixation on another person and the obsessive desire to establish and maintain a connection with them. The limerent individual's attention, emotional energy, and mental focus are often diverted away from their partner and/or children, creating emotional distance and relational instability. This can lead to considerable turmoil not only for the individual but also for those closest to them.

Limerence can also occur as a mutual phenomenon. In these instances, both individuals are infatuated with each other, yet external circumstances prevent the relationship from developing. These situations often evoke the timeless story of Romeo and Juliet, where deep longing exists on both sides, but barriers stand in the way. Common examples include two people who desire a relationship but face family disapproval, or individuals in existing partnerships who develop intense feelings for one another but remain constrained by their commitments. Such external limitations can heighten emotional intensity and prolong the state of limerence. Sustained by the powerful interplay of hope and doubt, these dynamics usually remain unresolved, suspended in ambiguity.

Tennov has suggested that limerent episodes may occur once in a lifetime or sequentially with different desired people, and that each episode generally lasts between 18 months and 3 years (Tennov, 1979). However, Wyant notes that limerence can persist for decades (Wyant, 2021). In cases of mutual limerence where a relationship is blocked by external barriers, the combination of ongoing hope and uncertainty can sustain the state for an extended period, making recovery particularly difficult.

The distress, pain, and suffering caused by limerence can be profound. Understanding limerence is essential for professionals working with clients who are struggling with it. By recognizing the signs and learning to distinguish limerence from healthy forms of love, therapists can offer appropriate interventions and meaningful support. This guidance is crucial in helping clients move toward more stable and fulfilling relational patterns. Additionally, understanding the origins and trajectory of limerence plays a key role in providing adequate support to those trapped in its grip. It is my hope that this book serves as a catalyst for further research into this complex, disruptive, and fascinating phenomenon.

References

American Psychiatric Association. (1952). *Diagnostic and statistical manual of mental disorders* (1st ed.). American Psychiatric Publishing.

American Psychiatric Association. (1980). *Diagnostic and statistical manual of mental disorders* (3rd ed.). American Psychiatric Publishing.

Azdajic, D. (2016). Longing for the transcendent: The role of love in Islamic mysticism with special reference to al-Ghazālī and Ibn al-'Arabī. *Transformation, 33*(2), 99–109. https://www.jstor.org/stable/90008864

Bradbury, P., Short, E., & Bleakley, P. (2024). Limerence, hidden obsession, fixation, and rumination: A scoping review of human behaviour. *Journal of Police and Criminal Psychology, 40*, 417–426. https://doi.org/10.1007/s11896-024-09674-x

Clarke, D. (2003). *Descartes's theory of mind*. Oxford University Press.

Descartes, R. (1996). *Meditations on first philosophy* (J. Cottingham, Trans.). Cambridge University Press.

Drescher, J. (2015). Out of DSM: Depathologizing homosexuality. *Behavioral Sciences, 5*(4), 565–575. https://doi.org/10.3390/bs5040565

Fehr, B., & Russell, J. A. (1984). Concept of emotion viewed from a prototype perspective. *Journal of Experimental Psychology: General, 113*(3), 464–486. https://doi.org/10.1037/0096-3445.113.3.464

Fletcher, G. J. O., Simpson, J. A., Campbell, L., & Overall, N. C. (2015). Pair-bonding, romantic love, and evolution: The curious case of *Homo sapiens. Perspectives on Psychological Science, 10*(1), 20–36. https://doi.org/10.1177/1745691614561683

Freud, S. (2002). *Psychopathology of everyday life*. Penguin Modern Classics.

Goldstein, E. B. (2004). *Connecting mind, research, and everyday experience*. Cengage Learning.

Goleman, D. (1996). *Emotional intelligence*. Bloomsbury Publishing.

LeDoux, J. E. (1998). *The emotional brain: The mysterious underpinnings of emotional life*. Simon & Schuster.

Lerner, J. S., Li, Y., Valdesolo, P., & Kassam, K. S. (2015). Emotion and decision making. *Annual Review of Psychology, 66*, 799–823. https://doi.org/10.1146/annurev-psych-010213-115043

Linehan, M. M. (1993). *Cognitive-behavioral treatment of borderline personality disorder*. Guilford Press.

Observer. (1977, September 11). Will limerence take the place of love?

Planalp, S., Fitness, J., & Fehr, B. A. (2018). The roles of emotion in relationships. In A. L. Vangelisti & D. Perlman (Eds.), *The Cambridge handbook of personal relationships* (2nd ed., pp. 256–267). Cambridge University Press. https://doi.org/10.1017/9781316417867.021

Plato. (1911). *Phaedo* (J. Burnet, Ed.). Oxford University Press.

Tennov, D. (1979). *Love and limerence: The experience of being in love*. Stein and Day.

Wakin, A. H., & Vo, D. B. (2008). Love-variant: The Wakin-Vo I.D.R. model of limerence. In Inter-Disciplinary.Net 2nd Global Conference: Challenging Intimate Boundaries. https://digitalcommons.sacredheart.edu/psych_fac/131/

Watson, J. B. (1929). *Psychology from the standpoint of a behaviourist* (3rd ed.). Lippincott.

Willmott, L., & Bentley, E. (2015). Exploring the lived-experience of limerence: A journey toward authenticity. *The Qualitative Report, 20*(1), 20–38. https://doi.org/10.46743/2160-3715/2015.1420

Wyant, B. E. (2021). Treatment of limerence using a cognitive behavioral approach: A case study. *Journal of Patient Experience, 8*, 1–7. https://doi.org/10.1177/23743735211060812

1 The First Taste of Love

Forming Attachment

Our first human experience typically begins within the protective confines of the womb, where we exist in a state of profound connectedness, free from anxiety or separation. After approximately nine months of gestation, we begin our transition into the outside world. In most circumstances, our first encounter in this new realm is with our mother. Ideally, we are born directly into her arms or gently placed onto her chest, allowing for immediate skin-to-skin contact. This early moment of physical closeness marks the beginning of our journey into relational life and lays the foundation for our capacity to form attachment.

As a newborn, we are entirely dependent on our mother or primary caregiver for survival. We seek nourishment by suckling our mother's breast or by relying on a hand to feed us from a bottle. At this stage, there is no clear perception of separateness; the infant experiences themselves as intrinsically connected to their mother or primary caregiver. Ideally, the caregiver intuitively responds to the infant's cues and provides comfort and regulation in response to their needs. This sense of unity and harmony is, in optimal circumstances, preserved throughout the early months of life. It typically remains intact until around 18 months of age, when the child begins to develop a nascent sense of individuality and separation from the caregiver (Brownell et al., 2007).

With the emergence of a nascent sense of self, separate from the mother, the infant begins their lifelong journey of relating to others through the framework of attachment. Despite this growing self-awareness, the infant remains entirely dependent on the caregiver for survival and is biologically predisposed to always remain attuned to them (Ostlund et al., 2017). In addition to providing nourishment, the caregiver serves as a vital source of touch, love, and connection. These elements are essential for the infant's holistic development and long-term wellbeing.

The profound bond between an infant and their caregivers is shaped, in part, by neurochemical processes (Wan et al., 2014). One of the key neurotransmitters involved in early attachment is oxytocin, referred to as the "love hormone" or "bonding hormone." Oxytocin is released in both the caregiver's and the infant's brain during nurturing and affectionate interactions such as breastfeeding, cuddling, and gentle touch. This hormone promotes feelings

DOI: 10.4324/9781003563747-2

of closeness, trust, and emotional connection, reinforcing the attachment between caregiver and child (Scatliffe et al., 2019).

Another important element of early attachment involves the neurotransmitter dopamine, which is associated with pleasure and reward. When a caregiver responds sensitively and promptly to an infant's needs and provides loving touch, it stimulates the release of dopamine. This reinforces the infant's motivation to seek comfort and closeness from the caregiver again. Over time, this cycle of responsiveness and pleasurable interaction strengthens the child's understanding that the caregiver is a reliable source of safety and support, promoting the development of a secure bond (Carozza & Leong, 2021).

Additionally, the stress response system plays a pivotal role in early attachment. When an infant experiences distress or fear, the brain releases cortisol, the primary stress hormone. A responsive caregiver who soothes and comforts the child helps regulate this stress response. Through repeated experiences of being comforted, the infant learns to trust that their caregiver can provide safety and relief in times of distress (Thompson & Trevathan, 2008).

Impact of Emotional Neglect

Social and emotional connectedness is a fundamental human need. Research has shown the critical importance of touch and love in infancy, revealing that the absence of these essential elements can lead to physical, emotional, and intellectual impairment (Rogol, 2020). A poignant example of the consequences of emotional deprivation can be seen in the experiences of infants raised in substandard Russian orphanages. In these environments, limited or non-existent physical contact and nurturing resulted in the development of *psychosocial dwarfism,* a syndrome characterized by delayed motor and intellectual development caused by severe emotional neglect. Deprived of being picked up, held, or caressed, these children exhibited stunted growth and failed to reach their expected developmental milestones, illustrating the lasting impact of unmet attachment needs in early life (St. Petersburg-USA Orphanage Research Team, 2008).

Human biology drives infants to seek the basic resources essential for survival, including food, water, sleep, and social connection. Among these, the formation of attachment to caregivers is especially critical, as it supports both physical survival and emotional development. From early on, infants are instinctively aware of their dependence on caregivers, which highlights the importance of receiving consistent nourishment, comfort, and emotional security (Sullivan et al., 2011).

Object Permanence

During development, the infant acquires what is known as *object permanence,* which refers to the understanding that objects and people continue to exist even when they are no longer visible. This milestone holds particular significance in the infant's relationship with their primary caregiver. The infant begins to realize that the caregiver can leave the room and still return, which marks an important step in the development of trust and emotional regulation (Piaget, 1954).

Although the caregiver's absence may initially cause distress, this response is a natural part of early emotional development. With repeated experiences of the caregiver consistently returning and responding to their needs, the infant gradually learns that separation is temporary and not a threat to the caregiving bond. This process helps the child internalize a sense of safety and predictability, which fosters emotional resilience. Over time, these reliable interactions support the development of a stable and trusting relational pattern by reducing anxiety during brief separations and enhancing trust in the caregiver's availability.

Attachment Theory

While Piaget was documenting this cognitive shift, psychologist John Bowlby was examining the emotional and behavioral responses associated with separation. In the 1950s, Bowlby emerged as a pioneering figure in attachment theory. He defined attachment as "the enduring psychological connectedness between human beings" (Bowlby, 1969, p. 194). Observing that infants often responded to separation from their primary caregivers with protest behaviors such as crying, clinging, and screaming, Bowlby proposed that these responses were rooted in evolutionary biology. He theorized that maintaining proximity to a caregiver increased the likelihood of survival and that the drive to seek closeness and avoid separation was an adaptive trait shaped by natural selection (Bowlby, 1969).

Bowlby argued that when a caregiver consistently meets an infant's needs and responds with sensitivity, the infant develops a reliable emotional bond that fosters confidence, emotional regulation, and a growing sense of autonomy. In contrast, when caregiving is inconsistent or unresponsive, this process may be disrupted, making the infant more vulnerable to patterns of relational insecurity (Bowlby, 1969).

In the 1970s, psychologist Mary Ainsworth expanded upon Bowlby's theoretical work through her empirical research known as the *Strange Situation*. In this observational study, Ainsworth assessed infants between 12 and 18 months of age during brief separations from and reunions with their caregivers. From these observations, she identified three primary attachment patterns: *secure, ambivalent–insecure,* and *avoidant–insecure* (Ainsworth et al., 1978). The *ambivalent–insecure* pattern, marked by heightened distress and difficulty settling upon reunion, is now more commonly referred to as *anxious attachment* (Levine & Heller, 2012).

Building on Ainsworth's work, Mary Main and Judith Solomon later identified a fourth classification, *disorganized-insecure attachment,* based on inconsistent and conflicted behaviors observed in their research (Main & Solomon, 1986).

Influence of Early Experiences on Adult Attachment Style

Early experiences of safety, responsiveness, and consistent emotional connection play a crucial role in shaping attachment patterns that persist into adulthood. When caregivers are reliably responsive and emotionally attuned, children are more likely to develop a secure attachment style (Ainsworth et al., 1978). This foundation of trust and predictability enables children to explore their environment with confidence and to form expectations of others as safe and dependable. Over time, these internalized expectations contribute to the ability to form stable adult relationships, express emotions openly, and seek support when needed (Levine & Heller, 2012).

The quality of the relationship between caregivers also significantly influences the development of attachment in infancy (Nicolaus et al., 2021). From a young age, children observe and internalize the relational patterns between their parents or primary caregivers, which shape their emerging models of love, connection, and emotional intimacy (Levine & Heller, 2012). Consistently supportive and nurturing dynamics foster relational security, while chronic conflict, emotional inconsistency, or neglect may contribute to the development of insecurity.

Attachment patterns established in early life influence how individuals relate to others, regulate emotions, and manage stress throughout the lifespan. These patterns inform a person's expectations of self and others, shaping their capacity to trust, form close bonds, and seek or offer support. The neurobiological processes associated with early attachment further reinforce these emotional templates, establishing a foundation for future relational and emotional functioning.

References

Ainsworth, M. D. S., Blehar, M. C., Waters, E., & Wall, S. (1978). *Patterns of attachment: A psychological study of the strange situation.* Erlbaum.

Bowlby, J. (1969). *Attachment and loss, Vol. 1: Attachment.* Basic Books.

Brownell, C. A., Zerwas, S., & Ramani, G. B. (2007). "So big": The development of body self-awareness in toddlers. *Child Development, 78*(5), 1426–1440. https://doi.org/10.1111/j.1467-8624.2007.01075.x

Carozza, S., & Leong, V. (2021). The role of affectionate caregiver touch in early neurodevelopment and parent-infant interactional synchrony. *Frontiers in Neuroscience, 14*, 613378. https://doi.org/10.3389/fnins.2020.613378

Levine, A., & Heller, R. (2012). *Attached: The new science of adult attachment and how it can help you find—and keep—love.* Jeremy P. Tarcher/Penguin.

Main, M., & Solomon, J. (1986). Discovery of an insecure-disorganized/disoriented attachment pattern: Procedures, findings, and implications for the classification of behavior. In T. B. Brazelton & M. W. Yogman (Eds.), *Affective development in infancy* (pp. 95–124). Ablex.

Nicolaus, C., Kress, V., Kopp, M., & Garthus-Niegel, S. (2021). The impact of parental relationship satisfaction on infant development: Results from the population-based cohort study DREAM. *Frontiers in Psychology, 12,* Article 667577. https://doi. org/10.3389/fpsyg.2021.667577

Ostlund, B. D., Measelle, J. R., Laurent, H. K., Conradt, E., & Ablow, J. C. (2017). Shaping emotion regulation: Attunement, symptomatology, and stress recovery within mother-infant dyads. *Developmental Psychobiology, 59*(1), 15–25. https://doi. org/10.1002/dev.21448

Piaget, J. (1954). *The construction of reality in the child.* Basic Books.

Rogol, A. D. (2020). Emotional deprivation in children: Growth faltering and reversible hypopituitarism. *Frontiers in Endocrinology, 11,* Article 596144. https://doi. org/10.3389/fendo.2020.596144

Scatliffe, N., Casavant, S., Vittner, D., & Cong, X. (2019). Oxytocin and early parent-infant interactions: A systematic review. *International Journal of Nursing Sciences, 6*(4), 445–453. https://doi.org/10.1016/j.ijnss.2019.09.009

St. Petersburg-USA Orphanage Research Team. (2008). The effects of early social-emotional and relationship experience on the development of young orphanage children. *Monographs of the Society for Research in Child Development, 73*(3), vii-viii, 1–262, 294–295. https://doi.org/10.1111/j.1540-5834.2008.00483.x

Sullivan, R., Perry, R., Sloan, A., Kleinhaus, K., & Burtchen, N. (2011). Infant bonding and attachment to the caregiver: Insights from basic and clinical science. *Clinics in Perinatology, 38*(4), 643–655. https://doi.org/10.1016/j.clp.2011.08.011

Thompson, L. A., & Trevathan, W. R. (2008). Cortisol reactivity, maternal sensitivity, and learning in 3-month-old infants. *Infant Behavior and Development, 31*(1), 92–106. https://doi.org/10.1016/j.infbeh.2007.07.007

Wan, M. W., Downey, D., Strachan, H., Elliott, R., Williams, S. R., & Abel, K. M. (2014). The neural basis of maternal bonding. *PLoS ONE, 9*(3), e88436. https://doi.org/ 10.1371/journal.pone.0088436

2   The Beginning of Suffering
Maladaptive Developmental Attachment

When caregivers are inconsistently available to meet an infant's attachment needs, the child may develop an *insecure attachment style*. One such style is *anxious attachment*, characterized by heightened sensitivity to separation and persistent concern about the availability of significant others. According to attachment theory, this pattern can emerge when caregivers are unpredictably responsive or display heightened anxiety around separation (Ainsworth et al., 1978).

For example, if a caregiver consistently shows excessive worry during the infant's attempts to explore or engage in play, the child may internalize this anxiety. Over time, this may lead to hesitation in exploring the environment and reduced confidence in independent activity.

Likewise, if a child returns from exploration and finds the caregiver emotionally unavailable or disengaged, the experience may reinforce fears of abandonment and increase the child's dependence on external reassurance. These early relational dynamics can disrupt the development of emotional security and hinder the child's ability to explore the world with confidence.

Anxious Attachment

In adulthood, anxious attachment may manifest through behaviors such as an excessive need for closeness, difficulty tolerating separation, poorly defined interpersonal boundaries, an unstable sense of self, fear of conflict, protest behaviors, manipulative tendencies, codependency, and a profound fear of abandonment (Levine & Heller, 2012). At the core of this attachment style is the belief that personal exploration, whether of the self or the external world, may jeopardize the stability of close relationships. Individuals with anxious attachment fear that turning their attention away from a significant other will result in emotional disconnection or abandonment. As a result, they may avoid autonomy in favor of constant reassurance, which can undermine both personal development and relational stability.

This underlying fear compels individuals to remain close to their partner and to ensure their continued presence, even at significant personal cost. Their self-concept, interpersonal functioning, and worldview may become shaped

DOI: 10.4324/9781003563747-3

by this persistent anxiety. In some cases, the fear of abandonment outweighs concerns for personal wellbeing, contributing to prolonged involvement in unhealthy or abusive relationships. Additionally, individuals with anxious attachment may inadvertently create relationship strain through behaviors such as emotional overdependence, intrusive closeness, or attempts to control their partner. These behaviors function as maladaptive efforts to manage or reduce the anxiety experienced within the relationship (Levine & Heller, 2012).

Avoidant Attachment

Another attachment style that may develop in response to caregivers' inconsistent or inadequate responsiveness is *avoidant attachment* (Ainsworth et al., 1978). This style functions as a defensive strategy aimed at protecting the child from further emotional pain caused by neglect or unavailability. At its core, avoidant attachment is underpinned by the belief that it is safest to suppress the need for intimacy and emotional closeness, as such needs are unlikely to be met and will lead to disappointment or rejection. By minimizing emotional expression and distancing themselves from others, individuals with avoidant attachment attempt to maintain a sense of control and emotional self-sufficiency in the face of relational unreliability.

Avoidant attachment may develop when a child engages in exploration and returns to find the caregiver absent, emotionally unavailable, or inconsistently responsive. Over time, the child learns to suppress expressions of attachment needs as a way of coping with the unpredictability of care. This attachment style often results in emotional distancing and self-imposed isolation, as individuals disconnect from their need for closeness to avoid further disappointment. Rather than seeking proximity to a significant other to maintain relational security, individuals with avoidant attachment tend to push others away. This distancing serves as a defensive strategy to protect against the vulnerability, pain, and perceived betrayal associated with unmet emotional needs.

In adulthood, avoidant attachment manifests as a reluctance to engage in genuine emotional intimacy with a significant other. Individuals with this attachment style may avoid discussing emotions, evade conflict, and exhibit hyper-independence and self-reliant thinking. They may feel discomfort with closeness or commitment, report feeling "suffocated" by their partner, and engage in distancing behaviors such as infidelity, frequently changing partners, or consistently initiating the end of relationships. A persistent belief in self-sufficiency and a reluctance to rely on others further reinforces emotional detachment (Levine & Heller, 2012). These patterns can create significant challenges in romantic and interpersonal relationships, as the emotional barriers they construct limit vulnerability, inhibit deep connection, and undermine the development of secure, lasting bonds.

These attachment-related behaviors in adulthood are influenced, in part, by early neurobiological responses formed through interactions with caregivers. In addition, the absence of consistent and responsive care can activate the body's stress response system, leading to increased levels of cortisol, the primary stress hormone, in the infant's brain (Ludmer Nofech-Mozes et al., 2020). Prolonged elevation of cortisol has been shown to negatively affect brain development, particularly in regions involved in emotional regulation and coping processes (Burghy et al., 2016). As a result, the infant may develop heightened anxiety and hypervigilance, becoming increasingly attuned to potential threats in the environment. These early biological adaptations may contribute to the emergence of insecure attachment patterns and emotional difficulties later in life.

A lack of consistent nurturing and emotional attunement in early childhood may also impede the development of neural pathways critical for emotional regulation and empathy. When these pathways are underdeveloped, children with maladaptive attachment patterns struggle to recognize, understand, and manage their own emotional experiences. Difficulties in processing emotions may also limit their capacity to empathize with others, which can contribute to challenges in forming healthy, secure relationships in later life (Burghy et al., 2016).

Anxious Attachment and Limerence

These early attachment patterns may shape not only interpersonal relationships in adulthood but also the ways in which individuals cope with emotional needs. Further research is needed to fully understand the relationship between limerence and insecure attachment styles, but existing studies suggest that limerence may be more prevalent among individuals with anxious or avoidant attachment patterns (Feeney & Noller, 1990). Those with an anxious attachment style may be particularly susceptible to limerence, as the two share several psychological characteristics. Both involve an intense preoccupation with securing emotional closeness, a heightened sensitivity to signs of reciprocation, and a deep fear of rejection or abandonment (Feeney & Noller, 1990). These overlapping features may reflect a potential link between anxious attachment and increased susceptibility to limerence.

For individuals with an anxious attachment style, the intense longing characteristic of limerence may feel familiar, as it mirrors early attachment experiences marked by inconsistency and unmet emotional needs. The yearning for a distant or unavailable other can reinforce unresolved desires for validation, affection, and emotional closeness. Some research suggests that individuals with an anxious attachment style may also be more inclined to engage in romantic or sexual fantasy, using imagined closeness to compensate for emotional insecurity in real-life relationships (Birnbaum, 2007). This tendency to idealize and fantasize about connection closely parallels the cognitive and emotional patterns observed in limerence.

During episodes of limerence, individuals oscillate between intense anxiety about potential rejection and a compulsive need to seek signs of reciprocation to relieve the anxiety. Perceived moments of connection or responsiveness from the desired other can temporarily soothe these fears, offering brief emotional relief, but in the absence of consistent or real interactions the limerent individual frequently turns to idealized fantasies of emotional or physical closeness as a coping mechanism. These fantasies may serve to regulate distress, offering a sense of imagined intimacy that compensates for the lack of tangible connection.

Avoidant Attachment and Limerence

Individuals with an avoidant attachment style may also be vulnerable to limerence, though through a different psychological pathway. Their tendency to avoid genuine intimacy and emotional vulnerability can lead them to retreat into fantasies and daydreams as a form of emotional self-protection. Limerence provides a way for avoidantly attached individuals to experience intense emotions and a sense of connection without the complexities and demands of an actual relationship. The idealized other functions as a psychological safe space, allowing them to express a desire for closeness and unity while avoiding the perceived risks associated with emotional engagement.

Avoidantly attached individuals struggle with emotional connection and intimacy in committed relationships. Research indicates that they may be more likely to engage in infidelity, a behavior that can be understood as a response to discomfort with closeness and vulnerability (Fricker, 2006). For these individuals, seeking fulfillment through fantasy or extradyadic relationships may feel more manageable and emotionally safe than navigating the demands of genuine intimacy. Such behaviors serve as a psychological defense, allowing the person to maintain distance while still experiencing aspects of connection. These escapist tendencies closely resemble the fantasy-driven dynamics of limerence, suggesting that avoidantly attached individuals may also be vulnerable to developing limerent obsessions.

Limerence as Maladaptive Coping Mechanism

Limerence may ultimately function as a maladaptive mechanism through which individuals with anxious or avoidant attachment styles attempt to cope with unresolved attachment wounds. In both cases, limerence offers an illusion of connection while allowing the individual to avoid the complexities, uncertainties, and emotional demands of real relationships. By substituting fantasy for authentic emotional engagement, limerence serves as a protective strategy that temporarily soothes attachment-related anxieties, but which ultimately reinforces patterns of disconnection and unfulfilled relational needs.

While limerence may offer temporary relief from attachment-related anxieties, it does not address the underlying emotional wounds. Instead, it perpetuates a cycle of distress and unmet needs. The intense emotions and idealized fantasies characteristic of limerence are detrimental to an individual's mental health, as they foster unrealistic expectations and emotional dependency.

Ultimately, limerence serves as a poor substitute for the authentic, reciprocal emotional connection that is essential for psychological wellbeing and healthy relationships.

Relying on limerence as a coping strategy can have significant long-term consequences for individuals with insecure attachment styles. Over time, this dependence on fantasy may hinder emotional development and reinforce patterns of relational dysfunction. For individuals with an anxious attachment style, the ongoing pursuit of validation through idealized fantasies may intensify emotional instability and interfere with the development of secure and balanced relationships. For individuals with avoidant attachment, reliance on fantasy to meet emotional needs may reinforce their detachment, allowing them to bypass the vulnerability required for genuine intimacy. This pattern results in persistent emotional distance and dissatisfaction within relationships, ultimately reinforcing the very disconnection they seek to avoid.

Repetition Compulsion

Limerence appears to mirror early attachment wounds, raising the question of why individuals are drawn to familiar relational patterns even when those patterns were painful or unfulfilling. One possible explanation lies in the phenomenon known as *repetition compulsion*; a concept originally introduced by Freud (Kahn, 2002). Repetition compulsion refers to the unconscious tendency to recreate situations that reflect unresolved childhood dynamics, particularly those associated with unmet emotional needs. Freud theorized that individuals engage in these repetitive patterns as an unconscious attempt to gain mastery over earlier experiences. By reenacting familiar emotional scripts, they implicitly hope to achieve a different and more reparative outcome that addresses the pain and unmet needs of the past.

Repetition compulsion can be understood in relation to the idea that, just as the body continuously strives for a state of homeostasis, the psyche may also unconsciously attempt to heal itself from trauma. Freud observed that individuals act out unresolved issues from their past without conscious awareness. He proposed that traumatic experiences are frequently relived through repetitive behaviors, dreams, and therapeutic encounters (Freud, 1975). These patterns may represent an unconscious effort to gain mastery over the original trauma, transforming passive experiences into active ones to reestablish a sense of control.

Attachment theory supports Freud's notion of repetition compulsion by highlighting how early relational experiences shape patterns of behavior in adult relationships. According to attachment theory, the internal working models developed in childhood consist of beliefs and expectations about relationships that are shaped by early interactions with caregivers. These models influence how individuals view themselves, others, and the dynamics of emotional closeness. As a result, individuals may be drawn to partners who reflect the emotional dynamics of their early caregiving experiences (Levine & Heller,

2012). For example, someone who experienced inconsistent or neglectful caregiving may repeatedly choose emotionally unavailable partners. Similarly, someone raised by anxious or intrusive caregivers may be drawn to emotionally intense or overinvolved partners.

The neuropsychological perspective enriches the concept of repetition compulsion further by illustrating how early experiences, particularly trauma or neglect, influence brain development and emotional regulation. Childhood adversity alters the brain's stress response systems (Ludmer Nofech-Mozes et al., 2020), increasing an individual's vulnerability to repeating relational patterns that mirror early traumatic experiences. For instance, someone who experienced emotional neglect may unconsciously seek out relationships that recreate this dynamic, reinforcing familiar but maladaptive emotional scripts.

This understanding may help explain why individuals with early attachment wounds are more prone to developing limerence later in life. The intense longing for an unavailable other, the constant monitoring for signs of rejection or validation, and the fantasy-driven, addictive elements of limerence closely reflect their early childhood attachment dynamics. These behaviors can be understood as maladaptive attempts to deal with unresolved attachment wounds by recreating familiar relational patterns in the hope of achieving a different outcome.

References

Ainsworth, M. D. S., Blehar, M. C., Waters, E., & Wall, S. (1978). *Patterns of attachment: A psychological study of the strange situation*. Erlbaum.

Birnbaum, G. E. (2007). Beyond the borders of reality: Attachment orientations and sexual fantasies. *Personal Relationships, 14*(3), 321–342. https://doi.org/10.1111/j.1475-6811.2007.00157.x

Burghy, C., Fox, M., Cornejo, M., Nelson, E., Noble, P., Singer, J., ... Davidson, R. J. (2016). Experience-driven differences in childhood cortisol predict affect-relevant brain function and coping in adolescent monozygotic twins. *Scientific Reports, 6*, Article 37081. https://doi.org/10.1038/srep37081

Feeney, J. A., & Noller, P. (1990). Attachment style as a predictor of adult romantic relationships. *Journal of Personality and Social Psychology, 58*(2), 281–291. https://doi.org/10.1037/0022-3514.58.2.281

Freud, S. (1975). *Beyond the pleasure principle* (J. Strachey, Trans.). W. W. Norton & Company. (Original work published 1920).

Fricker, J. (2006). *Predicting infidelity: The role of attachment styles, lovestyles, and the investment model* (Doctoral thesis). Swinburne University of Technology.

Kahn, M. (2002). *Basic Freud: Psychoanalytic thought for the 21st century*. Basic Books.

Levine, A., & Heller, R. (2012). *Attached: The new science of adult attachment and how it can help you find—and keep—love*. Jeremy P. Tarcher/Penguin.

Ludmer Nofech-Mozes, J. A., Jamieson, B., Gonzalez, A., & Atkinson, L. (2020). Mother-infant cortisol attunement: Associations with mother-infant attachment disorganization. *Development and Psychopathology, 32*(1), 43–55. https://doi.org/10.1017/S0954579418001396

3 How Do I Love Thee?

Archetypes of Limerence

Throughout history, human experiences and emotions have been symbolically expressed through archetypes, universal symbols, and motifs residing within the collective unconscious. Carl Jung, who introduced the concept of archetypes into psychology, described them as innate, primal forms reflecting fundamental aspects of the human psyche (Jung, 1981). These archetypes repeatedly appear in myths, folklore, fairy tales, dreams, art, literature, and contemporary storytelling, bridging diverse cultures and historical periods. Archetypes offer profound insights into human nature, illuminating the complexities of emotional life. Exploring these archetypal patterns deepens the understanding of powerful psychological experiences, such as limerence, by revealing the unconscious forces that drive them.

Jung conceptualized archetypes as central figures within his depth psychology, introducing symbolic representations such as the *Shadow*, the *Anima*, the *Animus*, and the *Self*, each reflecting core psychological dynamics within the unconscious. Building upon Jung's foundation, other scholars and authors expanded the concept of archetypes to offer diverse frameworks for understanding human experiences. Clarissa Pinkola Estés (1996), for instance, explored archetypes specifically within the feminine psyche, drawing from myths, fairy tales, and folklore to illustrate their influence on women's psychological and spiritual journeys.

Archetypes can be conceptualized and understood through numerous lenses and can emerge from virtually any cultural or symbolic source to offer insights into the unconscious realms of the psyche. One frequently used framework is the pantheon of Greek deities, which vividly embodies diverse emotional and psychological themes.

In exploring limerence through the lens of archetypes, it is fitting to begin with Eros, the Greek god embodying passionate desire, romantic longing, and erotic love. Eros provides a compelling representation of the emotional intensity and transformative power inherent in the limerent experience. Examining how Eros manifests in mythology, psychology, and symbolic art offers valuable insights into the dual nature of limerence as both a life-giving and overwhelming force.

DOI: 10.4324/9781003563747-4

Eros

The English language has only one word for love, while many other languages contain multiple words to describe its different forms. In Ancient Greece, love was perceived not as a singular concept but as a multifaceted phenomenon. The ancient Greeks recognized several distinct forms of love, each with its own unique characteristics and significance. These classifications are eloquently explored in Plato's *Symposium* (Waterfield, 1994).

Plato identified four primary forms of love: *Eros*, *Philia*, *Agape*, and *Storge*. Eros, associated with passionate and romantic love, embodies intense desire and a profound longing for physical and emotional connection. It encompasses the erotic and sensual dimensions of love, igniting attraction and fueling desire.

Limerence, in its essence, closely aligns with Eros. It is a passionate, all-consuming experience, serving as a powerful, energizing force that unlocks a floodgate of emotions and reveals previously uncharted depths within the psyche.

The intensity of limerence can be revitalizing and is intimately connected to the life-giving force of sexual energy. Eros may also manifest as a profound longing for union with the Divine, expressed through spiritual and devotional practices. The concept of Eros as a vital, life-giving force appears throughout diverse mythological traditions and within psychoanalytic discourse.

The term *Eros*, drawn from the Greek concept of love, was adopted by Freud in his psychoanalytic writings to denote the vital life force and sexual energy within the psyche. Freud (1989) described Eros as the instinctual drive toward creating and sustaining life and stated that civilization itself exists to support and nurture these life-giving impulses.

Due to its alignment with Eros as a life-giving instinct, limerence can become intertwined with other survival instincts. To the limerent individual, the need for connection with the desired other may feel as essential as the need for food or water. For this same reason, limerence can feel profoundly energizing and activating.

The life-giving, energizing, and activating qualities of limerence are vividly symbolized by the archetype of Eros. As the son of Aphrodite, goddess of love, and Ares, god of war, Eros encapsulates the dual nature of limerence, representing the intersection of beauty and violence, desire and pain.

A sculpture that vividly captures the revitalizing essence of Eros is *Psyche Revived by Cupid's Kiss*, created in 1787 by Antonio Canova (Figure 3.1). The sculpture portrays the moment when Eros revives the lifeless Psyche with a kiss. It symbolically illustrates the revitalizing and energizing force activated through limerence, powerfully embodied by the archetype of Eros.

Figure 3.1 Psyche Revived by Cupid's Kiss (*Psyché ranimée par le baiser de l'Amour*), 1787. Antonio Canova. Marble statue, 155 cm × 168 cm. Louvre Museum (Musée du Louvre), Paris. Photo: Jean-Pol Grandmont, 2011. Licensed under CC BY 4.0.

Eros and Psyche

The mythological tale of Eros (known as Cupid in the Roman pantheon) and Psyche reveals deep insight into the trajectory of limerence. According to Greek mythology, Psyche, whose name translates as "soul," was a mortal princess, the youngest and most beautiful of her sisters. Her beauty drew immense admiration and praise, so much so that it angered Aphrodite, the goddess of beauty and love, who felt neglected and overshadowed. Consumed by envy, Aphrodite instructed her son Eros to punish Psyche by shooting her with an arrow that would cause her to fall in love with the vilest and cruelest man on earth. Eros obediently set out to fulfill his mother's command, but upon beholding Psyche's exquisite beauty he was distracted and accidentally wounded himself with one of his arrows. Struck by his own spell, Eros instantly fell deeply in love with Psyche.

Eros took Psyche to his palace on Mount Olympus, where she would live in splendor and want for nothing. His sole condition was that his true identity remain hidden. He warned Psyche never to look upon his face. Psyche soon fell deeply in love with Eros, and each night the couple consummated their desire in complete darkness. By night they would entwine as passionate lovers, yet by day Eros would vanish, leaving Psyche alone and longing for him.

During a visit to the palace, Psyche's sisters, consumed by jealousy over her newfound fortune, planted seeds of doubt in her mind about her mysterious lover. They told her that he might be a serpent or a monstrous creature and that she might need to slay him. They urged Psyche to wait until her lover was asleep, arm herself with a knife, and illuminate his face with a lamp. Overcome by curiosity and doubt, Psyche followed her sisters' advice.

Psyche waited until nightfall and armed with a knife and an oil lamp, approached her sleeping lover. When she illuminated his face, she discovered that Eros was breathtakingly beautiful. Entranced by his beauty, Psyche failed to notice the oil dripping from her lamp. The hot oil spilled onto Eros, startling him awake. In shock and pain, he leaped from the bed and fled.

Psyche immediately regretted her action. Devastated by Eros's departure, she longed desperately for his return, but he did not come back. Consumed by grief and despair, Psyche wandered the earth relentlessly, searching for him day and night. Her profound longing resonated throughout the heavens and, upon hearing her anguished cries, Aphrodite took pity on her and resolved to help.

Aphrodite approached Psyche, urging her to rise and compose herself. She then presented Psyche with four arduous tasks, each meant to test her worthiness and offer a path back to her beloved Eros. The tasks included sorting an enormous pile of mixed grains overnight, gathering golden fleece from dangerous rams, retrieving water guarded by fierce serpents, and, finally, acquiring a box of beauty from Persephone in the underworld. Each challenge was daunting, but with the timely assistance of compassionate animals and other helpers, Psyche managed to complete them. Upon finishing the final task, however, Psyche's curiosity overcame her once again. Despite Aphrodite's explicit instruction not to open the box, she did so, inadvertently unleashing a powerful curse that caused her to collapse instantly into a death-like sleep.

At that very moment, Eros appeared and discovered Psyche lying unconscious on the ground. He swiftly revived her with a kiss. Reunited with her lover and forever transformed by her trials, Psyche was granted immortality, allowing her to join Eros as an equal. The couple was married, and this time their union held no secrets or restrictions. Psyche was finally able to fully see and know Eros as her divine husband (Johnson, 2009).

This myth is rich with symbolism that mirrors the experience of limerence. Initially, Psyche was unable to see Eros. Similarly, during limerence, an individual does not truly perceive the object of their desire. Instead, they idealize and elevate them onto a pedestal without genuine understanding of their true qualities or human imperfections. Attempts to move closer to the desired other may paradoxically lead to greater feelings of separation and emotional pain, as the other remains idealized, distant, and ultimately unknowable. This is symbolized by Psyche's ill-fated attempt to see Eros against his wishes, which results in his departure and furthers their separation. The profound longing and despair Psyche endures while wandering the earth in search of Eros mirror the intense yearning and relentless pursuit of signs of emotional reciprocation that is characteristic of limerence.

Aphrodite's decision to take pity on Psyche ultimately marks a pivotal shift in the narrative. Although it is Aphrodite, the goddess of love, who sets Psyche's suffering in motion, it is also Aphrodite, as the embodiment of love, who offers the path to healing. The tasks she assigns Psyche each offer a way out of longing and sorrow. Psyche is only able to complete these tasks with the assistance of animals, symbolizing the intuitive and healing instincts within human consciousness.

Psyche's story parallels the therapeutic journey required to overcome limerence. The final task, a descent into the underworld, symbolizes delving deeply into the unconscious mind where emotional wounds and trauma reside. Emerging safely from this journey with the box represents the attainment of conscious awareness. When Psyche opens the box, she falls into a death-like sleep, a moment that reflects how resurfacing trauma can initially manifest as emotional paralysis, depression, or numbness. Yet it is this very act that calls Eros back to her, allowing him to revive her and awaken her into fuller consciousness. Although opening the box initially brings suffering, as confronting emotional pain buried beneath limerent experiences often does, this act of facing the hidden trauma is ultimately life-affirming. It is precisely by illuminating these painful experiences and bringing them to the surface that genuine transformation and healing become possible.

Finally, Eros revives Psyche with his life-affirming kiss. She is at last able to see him clearly, and they are wed, becoming equals. This symbolic reunion represents the dissolution of limerence through gaining awareness of its underlying emotional and unconscious roots and bringing them into the light of conscious awareness. To truly see these once-hidden emotional wounds is to enable healing, profound transformation, and a movement towards healthy love.

Cupid's Arrow

The Greek god Eros was later adapted into Roman mythology as Cupid, the winged archer of desire (Johnson, 2009). In this later tradition, Cupid is portrayed as mischievous and unpredictable, shooting enchanted arrows into unsuspecting hearts and triggering sudden, overwhelming infatuation. This love is not gradual or logical, but rather immediate, consuming, and beyond conscious control.

The image of Cupid's arrow powerfully captures the involuntary nature of limerence. Just as Cupid's targets have no agency over whom they fall for, the limerent individual is overtaken by desire that arrives without warning or choice. The experience resembles enchantment: irrational, intoxicating, and emotionally disorienting.

The metaphor of the arrow also contains a painful duality. Cupid's arrows ignite desire while simultaneously inflicting a wound. This mirrors limerence, where the yearning for union brings moments of euphoria that are followed by emotional instability, uncertainty, and despair. The fantasy of connection exists alongside the ache of absence and unmet needs.

Psychologically, Cupid's arrow can be seen as a symbolic wound. The sudden impact does not only initiate infatuation; it also reactivates deeper, unresolved attachment wounds. In this sense, the new wound caused by limerence opens the doorway to older emotional pain that has been carried unconsciously. The desired other becomes a screen onto which the psyche projects unmet needs and unhealed longings, transforming them into the illusion of destined love or emotional salvation.

The myth also reflects the addictive and compulsive nature of limerence. In classical stories, those struck by Cupid's arrow become singularly fixated, behaving as though under a spell or in a trance. Their thoughts and actions revolve entirely around the pursuit of the desired other, with little regard for consequence or logic. This mirrors the compulsive focus of limerence, where the individual becomes psychologically and emotionally consumed, driven by a powerful craving, anticipation, and reward-seeking.

Cupid's arrow, then, becomes a symbol of both enchantment and entrapment. It evokes the illusion of fated love, the reactivation of early wounds and the unconscious search for healing through another. It illustrates the powerful pull of psychological addiction, where desire becomes fixation, and longing becomes pain.

Persephone

The myth of Persephone offers a potent archetypal lens through which to view the internal dynamics of limerence, particularly in relation to loss of control, descent into the unconscious, and the complex process of emotional integration. In Greek mythology, Persephone is the daughter of Demeter, the earth goddess, and is initially portrayed as an innocent maiden gathering flowers in a field. Her life is irrevocably altered when Hades, god of the underworld, abducts her and carries her to his shadowy realm to be his queen. Although Zeus intervenes and demands her release, Hades ensures her partial return by offering her pomegranate seeds, binding her to spend part of each year in the underworld. This mythic abduction marks the beginning of Persephone's transformation from child to sovereign, from innocence to consciousness.

In the context of limerence, Persephone represents the part of the psyche that is pulled into obsession and emotional intensity without conscious choice. Her descent into the underworld echoes the psychological spiral experienced by many limerent individuals, falling into a realm of longing, fixation, and emotional disorientation without full understanding or control. Just as Persephone is taken from her world and held in a place she did not choose, the limerent individual feels overtaken by emotions that are involuntary and confusing.

The duality of Persephone's experience is central to her archetypal significance. She is both victim and queen, captive and ruler. Similarly, the limerent individual oscillates between helpless surrender to emotional fixation and a deep attachment to the imaginary realm into which they have been drawn.

The cyclical nature of Persephone's myth, her annual return to the surface and descent back into the underworld, mirrors the emotional cycles of limerence. These include moments of ecstatic highs during perceived emotional reciprocity, followed by crashing lows during perceived rejection or emotional absence.

Persephone's eventual emergence as queen of the underworld speaks to the transformative potential embedded within the limerent experience. When the individual begins to examine the unconscious forces driving their obsession, such as attachment wounds, unresolved longing, addiction and unmet emotional needs, and learns to integrate these aspects of the psyche with compassion and awareness, they can reclaim their inner wholeness. What once felt like helpless captivity may evolve into insight, healing, and emotional integration.

Aphrodite

Aphrodite, the Greek goddess of love, beauty, sensuality, and seduction, represents the enchanting yet volatile aspects of romantic love. As an archetype she evokes desire, passion, and erotic magnetism, stirring emotional upheaval in those who fall under her influence. In the context of limerence, Aphrodite emerges as both a muse and a provocateur, luring individuals into experiences marked by intensity, longing, and emotional intoxication.

Aphrodite possesses a magnetic pull and represents an archetypal force that awakens the senses and calls forth vitality and erotic aliveness. She does not offer safety or predictability but thrives in the intoxication of passion and pursuit. Those who fall into her realm are swept away by the immediacy of desire, disregarding consequence, stability, or logic. In limerence, this manifests as impulsivity, intense desire, and the loss of self within the rapture of the imagined union.

Aphrodite's role in mythology frequently illustrates the duality of love's ecstasy and its capacity to destabilize. She inspires love affairs and erotic awakenings but also ignites jealousy, rivalry, and betrayal. Her presence is rarely subtle. Rather, she demands total surrender to the moment, often at the expense of clarity and restraint. In this sense, she mirrors the all-consuming nature of limerence, where emotional intensity overrides discernment and where the passionate pursuit of the desired other can become self-destructive.

The Aphrodite archetype is not concerned with deep union or long-term commitment (Bolen, 2014). She is devoted to transformation through erotic and emotionally charged experience. For the limerent individual, this archetype may emerge through the idealization of the desired other, who becomes infused with godlike qualities. Aphrodite is projected onto the desired person, who then becomes a vessel for experiencing her energy. At the same time, the limerent individual may feel themselves activated by Aphrodite's presence, especially in moments of heightened erotic intensity or creative inspiration.

This encounter with Aphrodite's energy can feel intoxicating and transcendent. Yet Aphrodite does not remain in one place. She is a transient force, igniting flames and then moving on. When the limerent bond is severed, her absence can feel like a fall from grace and a return from ecstasy into aching emptiness. In this way, her archetype illuminates both the power and the dangers of surrendering to limerence.

Despite her unpredictability, Aphrodite holds the potential for creative and spiritual awakening. She is the goddess who initiates transformation through beauty, sensuality, and passion. Her energy can catalyze profound change if integrated consciously rather than blindly pursued. The archetype, then, invites a deeper engagement with one's own erotic nature and capacity for connection. This process is not about projecting idealized love onto the desired other, but rather about reclaiming the path to inner wholeness and embodied sensuality within the self.

The Golden Apple

Throughout Greek mythology, Aphrodite is shown to crave attention and admiration. She becomes enraged when mortals fail to honor her and delights in the influence she wields. The tale of the golden apple illustrates her desire for recognition and power. According to the myth, Eris, the goddess of discord, throws a golden apple inscribed with "to the fairest" among the goddesses Hera, Athena, and Aphrodite. This sparks a fierce competition, with each goddess convinced she is most deserving of the prize.

Paris, a mortal prince, is appointed to decide who should receive the apple. Each goddess offers him a bribe. Aphrodite promises him the love of the most beautiful mortal woman, Helen of Troy. Seduced by the promise of irresistible beauty and romantic fulfillment, Paris awards the apple to Aphrodite. His choice ultimately triggers the Trojan War (Bolen, 2014).

This myth symbolically reflects the inner conflict present in limerence, a psychic struggle between competing archetypal forces. Aphrodite, with her devotion to beauty, sensual pleasure, and immediate gratification, represents the archetype within the psyche that fuels limerent obsession. In contrast, Athena, goddess of wisdom and strategy, symbolizes clarity, discernment, and conscious self-awareness. Hera, goddess of marriage and domestic order, embodies commitment, loyalty, and relational responsibility (Bolen, 2014).

These forces coexist in tension within the limerent individual. One part yearns for the intoxicating thrill of romantic ecstasy, the egoic high of being chosen, and the rush of idealized connection. Another part may recognize the potential harm, particularly when the limerent attachment threatens or betrays an existing relationship, commitment, or personal value system. In such cases, when the psyche grants the golden apple to Aphrodite, the consequences may extend beyond inner turmoil and spill into real-life conflict, broken trust, or moral dissonance. Just as Paris's choice led to war, the unchecked pursuit of limerent desire can create chaos both within and beyond the self.

The question of who receives the golden apple becomes a symbolic representation of which archetype dominates the psyche. When Aphrodite prevails, the individual may be overtaken by desire, idealization, and impulsive emotional pursuit. When Athena leads, reason and logic guide the individual toward clarity and discernment. When Hera rises to prominence, the focus shifts toward loyalty, honoring commitments, and preserving peace within existing relational structures. The myth, then, becomes an allegory for the psychological landscape of limerence, where desire, logic, and relational integrity continually compete for control, shaping the path toward either fragmentation or integration.

The Wounded Healer

As both a mythological figure and a Jungian construct, the Wounded Healer uniquely bridges the symbolic richness of Greek mythology with the inner psychic processes. Rooted in Greek mythology and later developed in Jungian psychology, this figure originates with Chiron, a centaur renowned for wisdom and healing abilities. Although capable of healing others, Chiron carries a wound that would never heal. This suffering becomes the source of deep compassion, enabling him to guide and support others even while remaining in pain himself.

In psychological terms, the Wounded Healer represents the aspect of the self that seeks to transform personal suffering into empathy, insight, and growth (Jung, 1966). It also reflects the paradox of being able to care deeply for others while remaining unable to fully heal one's own inner wounds. Within the context of limerence, this archetype may appear as an unconscious drive to soothe, rescue, or repair the emotional pain of the desired other. Attraction may form around those who appear emotionally unavailable or wounded, reflecting unresolved attachment patterns or early relational damage.

When an unhealed attachment wound is present, caregiving may be used as a strategy to create connection. Acts of love, emotional availability, and attentiveness are offered in hopes of generating intimacy or mutual healing. The desired other becomes the focal point of this effort because tending to the other activates the hope that love and care will finally be returned.

This outward offering, however, does not guarantee healing. When the desired other does not reciprocate, the result is emotional depletion. One-sided caregiving leaves the original wound unaddressed. Emotional effort may be misinterpreted as intimacy, sustaining a cycle in which care is given without receiving anything in return.

In its unconscious form, the Wounded Healer archetype may lead to emotional overextension, self-neglect, and ongoing disappointment. True healing does not emerge through rescuing another, but through turning inward and addressing the pain held within. What is ultimately required is not an idealized fantasy of connection, but a relationship grounded in mutual presence, emotional availability, and reciprocal care.

The Shadow

The Shadow is one of the most central and complex archetypes in Jungian psychology (Jung, 1981). It represents the unconscious aspects of the self that have been repressed, denied, or disowned. These are parts of the personality that we are unwilling or unable to acknowledge. Jung described the Shadow as the "hidden, repressed, for the most part inferior and guilt-laden" aspects of the psyche (Jung, 1959, p. 266). Although often perceived as negative or threatening, the Shadow is not inherently negative. It contains vital and creative energies that have been exiled from conscious awareness.

The Shadow becomes dangerous not because of its content, but because of its invisibility. When these disowned aspects of the self remain buried in darkness without the light of conscious awareness, they tend to fester. Over time they can distort thoughts, fuel emotional reactivity, and drive compulsive behaviors. The Shadow does not seek to destroy but rather to be recognized. Its disruptive manifestations are a plea for integration and for a place within the larger whole of the personality. Until the Shadow is seen and welcomed, it will continue to seek expression in indirect ways that can be destructive.

In the context of limerence, the Shadow reveals itself through the intensity of projection onto the desired other. The qualities the limerent individual attributes to the desired person are rarely grounded in reality. Instead, they arise from unconscious material that has been split off from the self. The desired other becomes a canvas for these disowned parts, including fantasies of completion, longed-for virtues, buried shame, unmet needs, and unresolved emotional wounds.

What makes this projection so powerful is that it offers a momentary sense of wholeness. The limerent individual unconsciously merges with an idealized figure who appears to embody everything they feel they lack, such as strength, sensuality, confidence, innocence, or vulnerability. In this way, limerence becomes a stage on which the Shadow can express itself, inserting these forgotten aspects into the drama of the psyche in an attempt to be seen, felt, and known.

The more deeply repressed the Shadow material, the more intensely it tends to express itself during limerent episodes. Emotions such as jealousy, anxiety, despair, and rage surface when the idealized connection begins to fracture or when the desired other remains emotionally unavailable. These reactions are heightened not only because of the immediate relational dynamic, but also because the psyche senses the threat of once again losing access to the projected shadow material.

The Demon Lover

One such shadowy figure within the psyche that is closely entwined with the experience of limerence is the Jungian archetype of the *Demon Lover*. Rooted in myth, literature, and depth psychology, the Demon Lover represents the seductive and destructive side of romantic obsession. This figure captivates the heart and mind through irresistible allure, promising bliss that remains forever out of reach. Feeding on the emotional energy of the limerent individual, the Demon Lover sustains itself through fantasies of union and reciprocity that never fully materialize (Woodman, 1993).

This archetype appears throughout history in literature and poetry. Writers such as Emily Dickinson, Emily Brontë, Sylvia Plath, and Virginia Woolf have portrayed this figure through themes of longing, surrender, entrapment, and loss. Their works reveal the push–pull dynamic of the Demon Lover, characterized by moments of intense connection followed by sudden withdrawal, creating a cycle of obsession in which the desired other always remains just beyond reach.

The allure of the Demon Lover is especially potent for those with histories of absent or inconsistent caregiving. In such cases, the psyche may attempt to resolve early attachment wounds by unconsciously recreating familiar patterns of longing, neglect, and abandonment. The Demon Lover becomes a symbolic projection of unmet emotional needs and a captivating yet destructive presence that dominates thoughts, feelings, and fantasies while feeding on psychic energy.

Thriving on illusion, the Demon Lover seduces the individual into believing that union with the idealized other will heal their inner emptiness. Yet each imagined reunion is fleeting, and every promise remains unfulfilled. Caught in this spell, the limerent individual gradually surrenders control, becoming ensnared in a self-perpetuating web of desire, fantasy, and despair. The Demon Lover does not offer genuine love or intimacy but instead mirrors the individual's deepest insecurities, reinforcing cycles of emotional deprivation and dependency.

While Eros activates the energizing and life-affirming qualities of limerence, the Demon Lover hijacks this energy and feeds upon it, functioning like a psychic vampire. It drains the individual's vitality while keeping them distracted through a constant stream of fantasies, projections, and imagined encounters. These seductive inner images create the illusion of intimacy and fulfillment, maintaining mental captivity as emotional and psychic resources are slowly depleted.

Like the vampires of myth and literature, the Demon Lover may be both feared and desired. Even as the individual is being drained, there is a simultaneous and irrational longing to remain close to the source of suffering. The attraction becomes inseparable from the pain, and the emotional dependency deepens.

During limerence, the true nature of the desired other is obscured by idealization. The individual becomes infatuated not with the real person but with a projection of their own imagination. The Demon Lover, as a false and alluring figure, embodies this fantasy. It shape-shifts into the form of the idealized other, reinforcing the illusion to continue feeding on psychic energy.

Under its influence, the limerent individual is drawn deeper into an imagined realm and further away from the reality of their life. Gradually and unconsciously, the limerent individual surrenders increasing amounts of psychic control, eventually becoming consumed by intrusive thoughts and obsessive fantasies. In this way, the Demon Lover traps the individual in a prolonged cycle of obsession, longing, and psychological captivity, as a way of perpetuating its own existence within the psyche.

Anima/Animus

Another archetype closely tied to the experience of limerence is the Anima/Animus, which represents the unconscious feminine and masculine aspects of the psyche. Traditionally, Jung described the Anima as the inner feminine within a man, and the Animus as the inner masculine within a woman. In contemporary understandings, however, these archetypes are seen as universal psychic structures present in all people, regardless of gender identity or sexual orientation. They reflect the full range of internal qualities that have not yet been fully recognized or integrated, such as intuition, rationality, sensitivity, assertiveness, and spiritual insight.

According to Jung, psychological growth involves bringing these inner opposites into conscious awareness. He referred to this as the individuation process, in which "the individual becomes what he always was," by integrating the fragmented aspects of the psyche into a cohesive and whole self (Jung, 1981).

The Anima and Animus are shaped by early relational experiences, through interactions with caregivers and significant figures. Over time, these inner images influence how we perceive others and how we relate to the complementary qualities within ourselves. Qualities we admire or idealize in others may reflect unclaimed aspects of our own inner life.

In the context of limerence, the projection of the Anima or Animus onto the desired other is common and emotionally intense. The limerent individual may unconsciously attribute idealized traits to the desired person, such as wisdom, creativity, strength, tenderness, or spiritual radiance. These projections are not necessarily grounded in who the other person truly is, but rather express disowned or unconscious parts of the self.

The intense yearning to merge with the desired other may represent the psyche's attempt to bridge inner opposites and move toward psychological wholeness. The desired person becomes a symbolic figure, carrying the energy of what is missing or underdeveloped within the self.

References

Bolen, J. S. (2014). *Goddesses in everywoman: Powerful archetypes in women's lives* (13th ed.). Harper Paperbacks.

Estés, C. P. (1996). *Women who run with the wolves: Myths and stories of the wild woman archetype*. Ballantine Books.

Freud, S. (1989). *Civilization and its discontents* (J. Strachey, Trans.; P. Gay, Introduction). W. W. Norton & Company. (Original work published 1930).

Johnson, R. A. (2009). *She: Understanding feminine psychology* (Revised ed., Kindle ed.). HarperCollins e-books.

Jung, C. G. (1959). *Aion: Researches into the phenomenology of the self* (R. F. C. Hull, Trans.). Princeton University Press.

Jung, C. G. (1966). *The collected works of C.G. Jung, Volume 7: Two essays in analytical psychology* (2nd ed., G. Adler & R. F. C. Hull, Eds. & Trans.; Bollingen Series XX). Princeton University Press. (Original works published 1928 and 1943).

Jung, C. G. (1981). *The collected works of C.G. Jung, Volume 9 (Part 1): Archetypes and the collective unconscious* (G. Adler & R. F. C. Hull, Eds.). Princeton University Press.

Waterfield, R. (Ed.). (1994). *Oxford World's Classics: Plato: Symposium.* Oxford University Press.

Woodman, M. (1993). *Emily Dickinson and the demon lover* [Audiobook]. Sounds True Recordings.

4 You Make Me Feel So High
The Neurochemistry of Limerence

While archetypes and mythology offer powerful symbolic insight into the experience of limerence, modern neuroscience reveals the biological mechanisms that underpin the phenomenon. Limerence is not only a psychological and emotional experience, but also a neurochemical storm that powerfully alters mood, perception, and behavior. Understanding the brain's role in limerence helps explain why the experience can feel so sudden, intense, involuntary, euphoric, devastating, and destabilizing. It also clarifies why releasing the attachment to the desired other can be so profoundly difficult.

Love has the power to lift the mind and body into a heightened state of emotional bliss, producing a natural high that rivals any substance-induced intoxication. The rush of excitement, elation, and perceived connection creates an experience that is euphoric and consuming. Flooded with powerful neurochemicals, the body responds with a surge of energy, focus, motivation, and urgency.

The physiological changes associated with love are intense. The heart races, fueled by a surge of adrenaline, providing a powerful rush of energy. Cheeks flush, a visible sign of heightened arousal, while pupils dilate, mirroring the intensity of pleasure. As anticipation builds, the heart beats faster, and breathing alternates between breathlessness and deep sighs, capturing the interplay of anticipation and delight. Love can also reduce appetite and disrupt sleep, suppressing the parasympathetic nervous system responsible for rest and digestion in favor of heightened arousal and frenzied energy. Love consumes, directing all focus and energy toward the pursuit of the desired other.

These physiological changes are orchestrated by the intricate interplay of neurochemicals involved in the emotional experience of love. Evolutionary theorists suggest that romantic love evolved in humans to promote bonding and increase the likelihood of successful mating (Fletcher et al., 2015). The state of being in love generates a powerful drive to connect with and remain close to the object of affection. The neurochemical and physiological responses that accompany this state work together to draw attention toward the desired other, motivating the pursuit of intimacy and emotional connection.

This pursuit, fueled by excitement, euphoria, and the intense desire to bond, may serve an evolutionary function by encouraging longer-term pair

DOI: 10.4324/9781003563747-5

bonding. Such bonds can help secure paternal investment in both mother and child, increasing the likelihood of survival and wellbeing for the offspring. In evolutionary terms, this enhanced stability, and care may improve the child's chances of thriving and, ultimately, reproducing, thereby contributing to greater reproductive success across generations.

There is no single brain structure solely responsible for emotional experiences. Rather, multiple brain regions and systems work together to shape perception of emotion, including the experience of love (LeDoux, 1998). While the precise neurological mechanisms that give rise to love are still not fully understood, research has identified several neurochemicals that play a central role in producing and sustaining this powerful emotional state.

Dopamine

One such key player is dopamine, a neurotransmitter associated with the brain's "reward system." During the early stages of romantic attraction, dopamine is released in high levels, contributing to sensations of pleasure, excitement, and heightened motivation to pursue the desired other (Fisher et al., 2005). This surge creates a euphoric and elevated state, reinforcing romantic interest and emotional fixation (Earp et al., 2017). Moments of perceived reciprocity, when affection seems returned, intensify this euphoria and further stimulate the dopamine system. It is this cycle of reward and emotional high that may fuel the exhilaration of limerence and drive the continued pursuit of romantic connection.

Dopamine plays a crucial role in motivation by creating a sense of pleasure as a reward for engaging in behaviors essential to survival, such as eating, drinking, sleeping, and socializing. It acts as an internal reinforcement system, encouraging the repetition of these activities by making them feel rewarding. In this way, dopamine helps ensure that basic needs are consistently met by linking them to pleasurable experiences (Lewis et al., 2021).

The brain's dopamine pathways can be hijacked by certain substances and behaviors, including cocaine, nicotine, alcohol, chocolate, and social media. Instead of receiving dopamine as a natural reward for engaging in healthy, survival-based activities, the brain begins to associate pleasure with these artificial stimuli. This reinforcement system is tricked into treating non-essential behaviors as vital, fueling compulsive patterns that can undermine long-term health and wellbeing.

The ongoing motivation driven by dopamine's short-term rewards can compel repeated engagement in harmful behaviors, even when their negative consequences are well known. The brain becomes trapped in a cycle where the pursuit of fleeting pleasure overrides long-term wellbeing.

Limerence, much like the early stages of romantic love, may trigger a surge of dopamine. When a limerent individual indulges in fantasies about their desired person, dopamine may flood the brain, producing a rush of exhilaration. Even the smallest sign of reciprocation, such as a fleeting glance or brief interaction, may release a cascade of dopamine that intensifies the euphoria. This heightened state may fuel a strong motivation to seek out further signs of interest and to remain immersed in fantasies of connection.

This intense craving for reciprocation can lead to an addictive attachment to the object of desire. Dopamine serves as a powerful driving force, reinforcing the pleasure and reward associated with indulging in fantasies or capturing the attention of the desired person. Over time, the limerent individual may find it necessary to think about the person more frequently to achieve the same level of dopamine-induced euphoria. This growing dependence on dopamine reinforcement may sustain the cycle of obsessive thoughts and fantasies, closely mirroring the neural mechanisms involved in addictive behaviors. In this way, limerence can resemble an addictive disorder, like substance addictions that compel individuals to chase the fleeting intoxication of the high.

Serotonin

Serotonin, a key neurotransmitter involved in mood regulation and emotional stability, has also been implicated in the emotional disturbances associated with love (Leonti & Casu, 2018). Often referred to as the "feel-good" chemical, serotonin supports overall wellbeing by promoting emotional balance and reducing anxiety. Disruptions in serotonin levels have been linked to mental health conditions such as depression, anxiety, and obsessive–compulsive disorder (Derksen et al., 2020). Although research on the neurochemistry of limerence remains limited, some studies suggest that individuals with lower serotonin levels may be more prone to obsessive thinking patterns, including those seen in limerence (Marazziti et al., 1999).

During the early stages of romantic love, research suggests that serotonin levels may drop (Zeki, 2007). This reduction is thought to contribute to the obsessive and intrusive thoughts that accompany intense attraction. In healthy relationships, these neurochemical changes typically stabilize as emotional security develops and the bond deepens, allowing serotonin levels to return to normal. In limerence, however, this stabilization does not occur. Instead, the emotional intensity remains suspended in a heightened, unresolved state. As a result, serotonin levels may remain low, prolonging obsessive thinking and mental preoccupation. This prolonged dysregulation is one of several indications that limerence is not simply an early stage of love, but a distinct psychological experience with its own neurochemical and emotional profile.

The fluctuating mood swings commonly observed in limerence may also be partly explained by serotonin's role in this state. When the desired person appears responsive, the limerent individual may experience a temporary increase in serotonin, creating a fleeting sense of relief or emotional stability. This can give the illusion that the connection is deepening or moving toward something more secure. In reality, this sense of progress is rooted in fantasy rather than in tangible mutual development, reinforcing the emotional volatility of the limerent experience.

This temporary serotonin boost may reinforce the pursuit of perceived reciprocation, as the limerent individual begins to associate those moments with emotional relief and elation. Over time, they may become increasingly dependent on these cues to maintain a sense of balance and stability. This may reinforce the craving for further contact or validation, deepening the emotional fixation. While more research is needed to fully understand the role of serotonin in limerence, it is possible that an underlying imbalance contributes to the persistence of the limerent state (Marazziti et al., 1999).

Oxytocin

Another key player in the neurochemistry of love is oxytocin, often referred to as the "love hormone." Oxytocin is released during moments of physical intimacy, such as hugging, kissing, and sexual activity, and plays a central role in bonding, and creating trust and emotional attachment. Oxytocin enhances feelings of closeness and connection, helping to deepen intimacy and strengthen romantic bonds (Kuchinskas, 2009).

Further research is needed to fully understand the role of oxytocin in limerence. Because limerence usually lacks genuine bonding or sustained connection with the desired other, exploring how oxytocin may be involved in this state could offer valuable insight. If a limerent individual can form a secure, reciprocated relationship with the desired other, the limerent state may begin to dissolve, giving way to secure attachment. This transition would likely involve the natural release of oxytocin during real-life physical interactions, such as hugging, kissing, and other expressions of affection within a grounded and reciprocal relationship rather than one based on fantasy or projection.

In the context of limerence, where there is little or no real-life romantic relationship or physical contact, it remains uncertain how oxytocin may be involved. While oxytocin is typically associated with bonding through physical intimacy, more research is needed to explore its potential role in fantasy and imagination. It is possible that oxytocin could be produced and released during imagined interactions, even without direct physical contact. When a limerent individual engages in fantasies about their desired other, this imagined closeness may trigger the release of oxytocin, intensifying the illusion of connection. If this occurs, it may further strengthen the emotional bond and deepen the sense of attachment, even in the absence of a reciprocal relationship.

Similarly, oxytocin may influence the limerent individual's perception of reciprocation. During moments when reciprocation is perceived, whether real or imagined, oxytocin levels may increase, creating a heightened sense of connection with the desired other. This perceived emotional closeness may further reinforce attachment and deepen the limerent individual's emotional investment in the imagined relationship.

Oxytocin not only supports bonding and connection but also plays a role in reducing stress (Carter & Porges, 2012). When someone is in love, oxytocin helps induce a calming effect by suppressing fear, anxiety, and negative thoughts. For the limerent individual, the release of oxytocin during fantasies about the desired other may offer temporary emotional relief, soothing anxiety, and creating a sense of comfort.

It is possible that the limerent individual begins to rely on fantasies of the desired other to regulate their own stress response. These imagined interactions may become a readily accessible and low-effort source of emotional relief, offering temporary respite from the pressures and anxieties of everyday life.

By immersing themselves in the imagined connection, the limerent individual may find temporary solace from emotional discomfort or internal tension. Fantasies about the desired other can become a dependable outlet for relief, offering moments of calm when other forms of coping are unavailable or ineffective. From this perspective, limerence can be understood in part as a dysfunctional coping mechanism, functioning as an attempt to manage distress through mental escape rather than by addressing its underlying causes.

Norepinephrine

Norepinephrine, a neurotransmitter involved in the body's stress response, also plays a significant role in the experience of love. It triggers physiological changes linked to heightened arousal and focused attention. During the early stages of romantic attraction, norepinephrine contributes to feelings of excitement and euphoria. It sharpens mental focus and increases alertness, intensifying emotional engagement and amplifying the sense of romantic urgency (Seshadri, 2016).

In the context of limerence, norepinephrine may help account for the heightened emotional arousal and physical agitation that characterize the experience. A surge of norepinephrine in the brain can lead to increased energy, elevated heart rate, and a heightened sense of vigilance. These physiological responses may intensify the obsessive nature of limerence, fueling a near-manic preoccupation with the desired other and a constant drive to seek out signs of reciprocation.

Endorphins

The potential role of endorphins in limerence also presents an intriguing area for further research. Endorphins are neurotransmitters that act as the brain's natural painkillers and mood enhancers, promoting sensations of pleasure, euphoria, and general wellbeing (Chaudhry & Gossman, 2023). Endorphin release may contribute to the emotional highs and feelings of elation involved in intense states like limerence. This biochemical reinforcement may further sustain the limerent state by making the presence or thought of the desired other feel emotionally and physically soothing.

While research on the specific role of endorphins in limerence is limited, existing knowledge about their effects on emotion and experience offers valuable insight. Endorphins are released in response to various stimuli, including physical pain, stress, exercise, and emotionally charged experiences. By binding to opioid receptors in the brain, they reduce the perception of pain and trigger sensations of pleasure and reward (Chaudhry & Gossman, 2023).

The intense emotions and excitement characteristic of limerence may stimulate the release of endorphins. The early stages of romantic attraction and the pursuit of a desired person are emotionally heightened, potentially activating the brain's reward system. This activation includes the release of endorphins, which may help explain why individuals experiencing limerence frequently report feelings of euphoria, joy, and a heightened sense of wellbeing when they feel emotionally close to the desired other.

Additionally, the obsessive nature of limerence may itself contribute to the release of endorphins. When individuals engage in behaviors such as fantasizing about the desired other or seeking signs of reciprocation, they may experience heightened emotional states like excitement and anticipation. These emotional responses can prompt the brain to release endorphins, reinforcing the pleasure linked to the limerent experience and sustaining the cycle of fixation.

Sex Differences

Investigating potential biological sex differences in the neurochemical processes of limerence is another important area of research that may provide valuable insights into how biologically male and female individuals experience and process romantic feelings differently. While individual experiences of limerence can vary widely, evidence suggests that hormonal and structural brain differences between the sexes may influence how these intense emotional states are experienced (Seshadri, 2016).

Hormones such as testosterone and estrogen play a significant role in shaping emotional and behavioral responses. Testosterone is associated with traits like assertiveness, dominance, and competitiveness. Research has explored its link to romantic attachment in males, with higher levels being associated with a preference for short-term mating strategies, and lower levels correlating with a tendency toward long-term commitment (Roney & Gettler, 2015). These hormonal variations may influence the intensity and duration of limerence in males. Conversely, lower testosterone levels, as commonly seen in females, have been linked to increased empathy and emotional attunement (van Honk et al., 2011), which may contribute to the deeper emotional bonding reported in limerent experiences.

Differences in brain structure and function between males and females may also shape how emotional experiences, including limerence, are processed and expressed. Studies have shown that males and females exhibit distinct patterns of activation in brain regions involved in emotional regulation, particularly the amygdala. The amygdala, which plays a central role in emotional processing, responds differently to emotional stimuli depending on sex (Andreano et al., 2014). These variations may influence both the intensity and quality of emotional experiences during limerence.

Additionally, research indicates that the left inferior frontal gyrus, a region of the prefrontal cortex involved in processing emotional information, shows different patterns of activation in males and females (Schirmer et al., 2004). These variations may reflect differences in emotional intensity and regulation, which could influence how limerence is experienced.

Neurochemical Effect

Limerence is characterized by intense emotional highs, including euphoria, stress relief, passion, and surges of joy and energy which are driven by fantasies and idealized connection. As a result, the limerent individual may become addicted to these feelings, continually seeking to sustain the flow of "feel-good" neurochemicals associated with the experiences. These emotional highs occur within the realm of fantasy and imagined connection, lacking any tangible or lasting impact on the individual's life, sense of self, or authentic connection to the world.

When the limerent individual is inevitably faced with reality, they are confronted with the painful truth that their fantasies of love and connection exist solely in their own mind. Any perceived rejection from the desired other, whether real or imagined, shatters the exhilarating highs of limerence, plunging them into deep emotional lows. In these moments, a wave of depression, heartbreak, and a profound sense of worthlessness may overwhelm them. This emotional turmoil likely stems from the sudden decline in the neurochemicals that were once elevated during their vivid fantasies of connection.

The limerent individual becomes consumed by an unrelenting craving to reestablish connection with the desired other. Compulsively, they immerse themselves in obsessive fantasies, driven by an insatiable need to recapture the intense euphoria once felt. Their pursuit takes on a frantic urgency, like an addict rummaging through the depths of a drawer in search of their next fix. Any form of perceived reciprocation is desperately sought, in the hope of reigniting the intoxicating high they have lost and powerfully crave.

The brain's reward system, which initially produces feelings of euphoria and joy, eventually becomes a source of distress for the limerent individual. During the low points of limerence, when dopamine and serotonin levels plummet, the individual becomes increasingly desperate for signs of emotional reciprocation. This desperation drives them to search feverishly for any indication, no matter how subtle or imagined, that the desired other may share their feelings. Even the faintest hint of reciprocation may trigger a rush of dopamine, offering temporary relief from the emotional low and reigniting the euphoric high they crave.

This neurochemical cycle of emotional highs and lows may create a powerful reinforcement loop in which the brain continually seeks out chemical surges to restore emotional balance. Over time, the limerent individual may become addicted to the neurochemicals driving these fluctuations, much like someone dependent on substances for relief. This pursuit of emotional reward locks them into a compulsive cycle of craving, making it increasingly difficult to let go and move forward.

References

Andreano, J. M., Dickerson, B. C., & Barrett, L. F. (2014). Sex differences in the persistence of the amygdala response to negative material. *Social Cognitive and Affective Neuroscience, 9*(9), 1388–1394. https://doi.org/10.1093/scan/nst127

Carter, C. S., & Porges, S. W. (2012). The biochemistry of love: An oxytocin hypothesis: Science & Society Series on Sex and Science. *EMBO Reports, 14*(12), 12–16. https://doi.org/10.1038/embor.2012.191

Chaudhry, S. R., & Gossman, W. (2023, April 3). Biochemistry, endorphin. In *StatPearls* [Internet]. StatPearls Publishing. Retrieved from https://www.ncbi.nlm.nih.gov/books/NBK470306/

Derksen, M., Feenstra, M., Willuhn, I., & Denys, D. (2020). The serotonergic system in obsessive-compulsive disorder. In C. P. Müller & K. A. Cunningham (Eds.), *Handbook of Behavioral Neuroscience* (Vol. 31, pp. 865–891). Elsevier. https://doi.org/10.1016/B978-0-444-64125-0.00044-X

Earp, B. D., Wudarczyk, O. A., Foddy, B., & Savulescu, J. (2017). Addicted to love: What is love addiction and when should it be treated? *Philosophical Psychology, 24*(1), 77–92. https://doi.org/10.1353/ppp.2017.0011

Fisher, H., Aron, A., & Brown, L. L. (2005). Romantic love: An fMRI study of a neural mechanism for mate choice. *The Journal of Comparative Neurology, 493*(1), 58–62. https://doi.org/10.1002/cne.20772

Fletcher, G. J. O., Simpson, J. A., Campbell, L., & Overall, N. C. (2015). Pair-bonding, romantic love, and evolution: The curious case of *Homo sapiens*. *Perspectives on Psychological Science, 10*(1), 20–36. https://doi.org/10.1177/1745691614561683

Kuchinskas, S. (2009). *The chemistry of connection: How the oxytocin response can help you find trust, intimacy, and love*. New Harbinger Publications.

LeDoux, J. E. (1998). *The emotional brain: The mysterious underpinnings of emotional life*. Simon & Schuster.

Leonti, M., & Casu, L. (2018). Ethnopharmacology of love. *Frontiers in Pharmacology, 9*, 567. https://doi.org/10.3389/fphar.2018.00567

Lewis, R. G., Florio, E., Punzo, D., & Borrelli, E. (2021). The brain's reward system in health and disease. *Advances in Experimental Medicine and Biology, 1344*, 57–69. https://doi.org/10.1007/978-3-030-81147-1_4

Marazziti, D., Akiskal, H. S., Rossi, A., & Cassano, G. B. (1999). Alteration of the platelet serotonin transporter in romantic love. *Psychological Medicine, 29*(3), 741–745. https://doi.org/10.1017/s0033291798007946

Roney, J. R., & Gettler, L. T. (2015). The role of testosterone in human romantic relationships. *Current Opinion in Psychology, 1*, 81–86. https://doi.org/10.1016/j.copsyc.2014.11.003

Schirmer, A., Zysset, S., Kotz, S. A., & von Cramon, D. Y. (2004). Gender differences in the activation of inferior frontal cortex during emotional speech perception. *NeuroImage, 21*(3), 1114–1123. https://doi.org/10.1016/j.neuroimage.2003.10.048

Seshadri, K. G. (2016). The neuroendocrinology of love. *Indian Journal of Endocrinology and Metabolism, 20*(4), 558–563. https://doi.org/10.4103/2230-8210.183479

van Honk, J., Schutter, D. J., Bos, P. A., Kruijt, A. W., Lentjes, E. G., & Baron-Cohen, S. (2011). Testosterone administration impairs cognitive empathy in women depending on second-to-fourth digit ratio. *Proceedings of the National Academy of Sciences of the United States of America, 108*(8), 3448–3452. https://doi.org/10.1073/pnas.1011891108

Zeki, S. (2007). The neurobiology of love. *FEBS Letters, 581*(14), 2575–2579. https://doi.org/10.1016/j.febslet.2007.03.094

5 I Love You So Much It Hurts
Longing and Compulsion

Mythologies of Desire

The neurochemical intensity of limerence may help to explain its compulsive nature, but it cannot fully account for the depth of longing it evokes. Beyond the brain's circuitry lies a force that feels ancient and mysterious, a yearning for union, wholeness, and a return to something that seems lost or incomplete. Limerence is a psychological state rooted in neurochemical processes, but it is also an expression of profound longing that reaches into myth, meaning, spirituality, and the hidden threads within the psyche.

At its core, limerence is a manifestation of desire. Desire is a powerful force. Some mystical traditions present desire as the force that moved the creator to create the universe. It is depicted as the energy that sparks creation. For example, in the Jewish mystical Kabbalistic tradition, there is a concept known as *tzimtzum*, which refers to the idea that God, as an infinite being without end, had to first contract in on Himself to make room for creation (Vital, n.d.). The reason given for this contraction is that God wanted, or desired, to create the universe. Thus, according to this tradition, desire becomes the most potent force of all, as it is the energy that initiates creation.

In Kabbalistic thought, desire is also understood as the force that unites humanity with the Divine. In this tradition, the Hebrew word *ratzon*, meaning will or desire, refers both to the Divine longing that initiated creation and to the yearning within the human soul to return to its source. This impulse originates in the Divine and flows through the individual, acting as a sacred drive toward closeness with God. Human desire becomes a manifestation of this divine energy, drawing the soul toward reunion with the One. In this sense, human desire transcends survival instincts and becomes a bridge to the sacred.

Similarly, in Hindu philosophy, *kama*, the third of the four *purusharthas* or aims of life, is understood as desire. While *kama* encompasses all forms of longing, sexual pleasure is considered a particularly vital aspect. It is seen as both a cosmic and a human energy, one that animates life and holds it in place. In Hinduism, *kama* is personified as Kamadeva, the god who triggers desire. This tradition presents desire as essential to life and its fulfillment as a duty to oneself (Das, 2018).

DOI: 10.4324/9781003563747-6

Similarly, in the Islamic mystical Sufi tradition, desire is deeply linked to divinity through the concept of *ishq*, a passionate, burning love for God that compels the soul toward union with the Divine. The Sufi tradition teaches that God created the universe out of love, longing for His creation to know Him. This divine longing, much like human desire, is seen as a creative force that not only initiates creation but also draws the soul toward closeness with God. In the works of Sufi poets like Rumi, *ishq* is portrayed as both a human and cosmic energy that connects the seeker to the Divine, moving beyond the limitations of the physical world and merging human longing with divine purpose (Bosworth et al., 1997).

On the human level, the act of procreation often begins with desire. As with Eros, the life-force energy, there is a continuous thread that links desire with creation. In this way, desire is a life-affirming energy that initiates and propels creative acts of bringing something into being. The same holds true for artistic expression. A painting, a song, or a piece of literature begins with the spark of desire to express, reflect, or create something. Desire is also a primal force linked to life and survival. Water is desired when thirst arises, food when hunger is felt, and connection when one feels alone. Desiring, wanting, longing, and yearning may therefore be conceptualized as natural, spiritual, and creative forces that animate life.

On the other hand, many traditions warn against unchecked desire. The story of the serpent and the apple in the Book of Genesis (the first book of the Hebrew Bible and the Christian Old Testament) is interpreted as a cautionary tale against giving in to temptation or desire. In the story, God presents His creation to Adam and tells him he can enjoy every part of it but warns him not to eat the fruit from the tree of the knowledge of good and evil. The serpent then seduces Eve into eating from the forbidden tree, and she shares the fruit with Adam. This giving in to temptation, sometimes referred to as *original sin*, leads to the humans' banishment from Eden to prevent them from eating from the tree of life and becoming immortal (Scherman, 1996). This act of disobedience and of giving in to desire, according to the Genesis narrative, is the beginning of human suffering. This suffering is longing, pain, and wanting but not having. It involves a separation from God, banishment from Eden, working with the sweat of one's brow to plant fields for food, and pain in childbirth, another symbol of the consequences of yielding to desire.

In Catholicism, desire is viewed with caution, particularly *concupiscence*, strong sexual desire or lust, which is seen as part of the fallen human condition resulting from original sin. According to this tradition, desire, when uncontrolled, can draw people away from God and moral purity. Catholic virtues such as chastity, temperance, and self-control are therefore encouraged to help individuals regulate desire to grow spiritually (Miller, 1993). Through practices like asceticism, saints and monks renounce worldly pleasures to reign in desire and strengthen their connection with God.

Similarly, Buddhism teaches that desire, particularly *tanha*, craving, is one of the core causes of suffering, as outlined in the Four Noble Truths (Harvey,

2013). According to this tradition, attachment to desires, whether material or emotional, leads to *dukkha*, suffering. The path to enlightenment involves letting go of desire, allowing individuals to transcend the cycle of suffering through the practice of non-attachment, mindfulness, and ethical living.

These conflicting perceptions of desire highlight its complexity. Throughout various mythologies and religions, desire is portrayed as both divine and human. It is a powerful force, capable of sparking the creation of the universe and driving the soul toward God, yet it is also a flaw, weakening the human psyche and distancing one from the Divine. Desire is then both the precondition for creation and the eternal cause of human suffering.

Human Longing

On an individual level, the cosmic force of desire is mirrored in daily experiences of longing and attachment. Just as spiritual traditions speak of the soul's yearning for unity and divine connection, personal longing for attachment reflects this universal desire for oneness. Desire arises from separation: That which is lacking becomes the object of yearning. In the same way that God was led to creation by the desire for something outside of Himself, human beings are drawn toward connection with others who exist beyond the self.

Human longing for closeness emerges with the earliest experience of separation. The infant slowly experiences more and more separation after birth. In this space, desire begins to take shape as a yearning for nourishment, contact, and recognition. This early imprint lingers throughout life, subtly shaping the patterns of longing, connection, and the search for closeness.

Inevitably, not every desire or need will be met in childhood. Even those with loving and consistently available caregivers will not have every need or want met. Some desires are not healthy for an individual, and it is not beneficial to have every desire granted. Learning to temper desire when appropriate is important for social learning and development. For example, a child may want another child's toy and must be taught not to snatch it and learn to sit with the discomfort of wanting something and not having it.

Some desires, such as the desire for safety, nourishment, and continuous emotional connection, are vital for healthy development. These needs are unmet to varying degrees across individual experiences. When a desire for connection or emotional safety is not met, a child will generally turn to substitutes to self-soothe. For example, a child or adolescent without access to an emotionally available caregiver may turn to distraction, schoolwork, food, substances, social media, television, online gaming, other relationships, self-harm, or dissociation as attempts to manage the pain of wanting but not receiving nourishing connection. These substitutes may change over time, but the act of substitution in place of connection persists into adulthood and can result in compulsive and addictive behaviors.

Beyond the behavioral patterns that arise from unmet longing, there is an emotional tension embedded within the experience of desire itself. Longing contains a sense of aversion, including fear that the desired object or outcome will remain out of reach. Aversion may also arise toward the state of wanting itself. Neediness can be uncomfortable to acknowledge. Desire shifts attention to something external, something not currently present, and directs focus toward a different state of being, having, or feeling. This disrupts the ability to fully inhabit the present moment with ease and acceptance, creating a deeper sense of discomfort or pain.

When attention is consumed by wanting, perspective narrows. Focus centers on a single absent thing, imagined as the key to fulfillment. In the experience of limerence, that fixation is directed toward another person. The desire is for that person to reciprocate affection, to offer love and closeness, so that the ache of longing might dissolve, and a sense of completion emerge. The belief forms that having this one person will create wholeness. Yet, as with other cravings or compulsions, the feeling of wholeness continues to elude the individual who seeks it in those places.

One way to conceptualize this is through the idea of the *hungry ghost*, a Buddhist concept depicting people who are driven by an insatiable internal desire to fill themselves up. Those driven by the hungry ghost are never satisfied, as they are unable to truly fill the void within (Gethin, 1998). If people are unaware of their true desires or longings, such as the desire for nourishing connection, they may try to continuously quench this longing with substitutes that never truly satisfy. This can trap individuals in patterns of compulsive and addictive behaviors.

Misdirected Longing

Limerence is an example of insatiable and misplaced wanting. During limerence, longing becomes intense and all-consuming, permeating the individual's entire being. It manifests psychologically as a yearning for closeness, physically as a pain in the chest, and emotionally as feelings of emptiness, frustration, and sadness (Wyant, 2021). It is a persistent state of wanting without having, of desiring someone who is absent. The fixation centers on the desire to be loved and wanted in return, driven by the hope that connection will bring relief or a sense of completion.

This pattern of longing may feel strangely familiar, even comforting in its pain, as it can mirror early emotional templates. The desired other becomes a symbol, a stand-in for the comfort, attunement, or belonging that once felt out of reach. Beneath the fixation lies a deeper yearning, not only for connection with another, but for a sense of wholeness that transcends the person. In this light, limerence may be understood as a form of emotional or spiritual misrecognition, a projection of an inner longing for connection that is both human and divine.

Perhaps it is when this innate desire for union is misdirected that longing becomes painful. This misdirection may be what spiritual traditions that warn against desire are referring to: not the desire itself, but the misunderstanding of it and the entanglement of longing with an unsatisfying external substitute. As the desire intensifies, so does the drive to seek fulfillment in places that cannot provide it, leading to patterns of behavior that become increasingly difficult to control.

Compulsive Behaviors

Longing, as experienced in the body, is uncomfortable. By definition it implies absence, not having something deeply wanted, which feels painful and unsettling. As a species, the instinct to seek pleasure and avoid pain is wired for survival and continuity. When discomfort or pain is experienced, such as the pain of longing, the natural instinct is to either avoid or resolve it.

When longing is as intense as it is during limerence, avoiding or distracting from the discomfort becomes difficult. The only option is to attempt to soothe it. Naturally, people attempt to soothe their longing for connection by trying to get their attachment needs met. This is when compulsive behaviors can begin to develop and take hold.

During limerence, the desired other is usually distant or unavailable, making it difficult for the limerent individual to have their need for closeness and intimacy met. With no or limited access to direct connection, they are left with no choice but to turn to indirect or roundabout methods of creating the illusion of closeness to soothe the discomfort of longing.

When these methods successfully create an illusion of connection, they may soothe longing temporarily, offering the limerent individual fleeting relief. This brief comfort reinforces the likelihood that they will repeat these behaviors whenever longing resurfaces. Over time, they may come to rely on these substitute behaviors to ease their suffering, establishing compulsive behavioral loops.

One example is the compulsive checking of the desired other's online status through messaging apps like Messenger or WhatsApp. Even without direct communication, the act of monitoring their last active status provides a momentary sense of connection for the limerent individual. This tenuous connection soothes their longing briefly, offering a short reprieve from the intense obsession and discomfort.

Another example is the continuous pursuit of connection with individuals associated with the desired person. When direct contact is limited, the limerent individual may go to great lengths to connect with people who are linked to the desired other. This behavior stems from a compulsive need to maintain any form of connection, even indirectly, to the desired other to soothe their longing. Here, the focus remains solely on using these connections as a way of feeling closer to the desired other rather than valuing the relationships themselves.

Such behaviors create complex and challenging dynamics. The limerent individual may view these associated people more as conduits to the desired other than as separate individuals. This may lead to strained relationships, as the motivations of the limerent individual may ultimately appear manipulative or insincere. In their obsessive need for connection, they may struggle to respect boundaries, prioritizing soothing their longing above the preferences and emotions of others.

Online searching is a common compulsive behavior during limerence. The limerent individual may spend hours googling the desired person or examining their social media activity, experiencing this as a form of connection. By studying their digital footprint, they may believe they are gaining insight into the person's thoughts, habits, or emotional state. This creates only an illusion of closeness, offering temporary satisfaction for their intense curiosity and longing without providing genuine engagement.

Rereading old emails or text messages is another behavior that can become compulsive when it offers momentary relief. Even mundane or neutral exchanges are revisited repeatedly to recreate emotional closeness or uncover new significance. The limerent individual may also listen compulsively to music associated with the desired person, particularly songs that evoke shared moments, imagined meaning, or emotional resonance.

While these compulsive behaviors may provide short-term relief, they ultimately reinforce attachment and perpetuate the cycle of suffering. They offer only a fleeting sense of control and satisfaction and prevent the limerent individual from breaking free from the grip of longing and discomfort.

Longing for Reciprocation

During limerence, an individual craves closeness with the desired person and longs for emotional reciprocation. The emotional attachment to the desired other becomes so intense that mood and behavior hinge on the pursuit of connection and evidence of reciprocation of feeling (Wyant, 2021). Any perceived rejection or withdrawal from the desired other can lead to feelings of heartbreak, low self-esteem, depression, and even suicidal ideation (Willmott & Bentley, 2015). To maintain the illusion of connection and minimize longing, the limerent individual constantly searches for signs of reciprocation.

The perceived level of reciprocation is often based on neutral or subtle behaviors that would likely go unnoticed by anyone not experiencing limerence. These perceived "signs" are rarely objective indicators of the other person's feelings and are imagined or embellished by the limerent individual, who obsessively attempts to decode and assign emotional weight to them.

For example, if a person is limerent for a barista who serves them coffee every morning, a brief conversation one day might elate them, leading them to believe their feelings are reciprocated and triggering a flood of fantasies and euphoria. If the barista doesn't engage in conversation the following day, though, the limerent individual may interpret it as a sign of rejection, causing an acute dip in mood and self-esteem.

Whether or not a simple, casual conversation takes place during an exchange of coffee can have a significant effect on the limerent individual's mood, outlook, behavior, and overall functioning for the day or week. In reality, the barista may be completely unaware of the limerent feelings and, to an outsider, both interactions would seem neutral and without emotional implication.

Similarly, if a limerent individual notices the desired person making eye contact during a conversation at the office, they may experience a rush of euphoria, interpreting it as a sign of reciprocated feelings. If eye contact is absent during their next interaction, though, they may perceive it as emotional withdrawal, triggering a sharp drop in mood. This shift can lead to a spiral of self-critical thoughts and make it difficult to focus on work or maintain connection in other relationships. Their ability to function may feel suspended until they receive another perceived sign of reciprocation, which is often imagined or exaggerated.

If the desired person engages with the limerent individual on social media, for example, by liking a story, it may bring a brief sense of peace, joy, and connection, but if there is no engagement for some time their mood may drop, and anxiety and obsessive thoughts may begin to intensify. This absence is interpreted as a withdrawal of affection. Their emotional state and daily functioning usually do not improve until they perceive another sign of reciprocation, no matter how small or ambiguous.

In some cases, even the "last online" status of the desired person can be interpreted as a sign of reciprocation, either positively or negatively. Although their online activity on messaging apps likely has nothing to do with the limerent individual, it may still be perceived as emotionally significant. The limerent person may interpret this activity as a reflection of interest, avoidance, or emotional withdrawal, despite there being no actual connection.

Seeking information from mutual acquaintances about the desired person is also common during limerence. The limerent individual may hope to glean any hint of reciprocation or emotional resolution. This ongoing search for "signs" can become compulsive, consuming their attention and causing shifts in mood based on how they interpret even small or ambiguous pieces of information.

The limerent individual's heightened sensitivity and selective perception lead them to assign significant meaning to these "signs", even when there is no objective basis. Subtle indications of rejection can trigger despair, resulting in emotional pain, heartbreak, or depression. They may begin to question their self-worth, reinforcing obsessive thought loops that intensify emotional turmoil and deepen the longing for emotional reciprocation.

Intermittent Reinforcement

The compulsive behaviors that limerent individuals engage in as an attempt to soothe their longing tend to fuel the obsession further due to intermittent reinforcement. Sporadic rewards sustain behavior more effectively than consistent rewards (Skinner, 1938). This principle helps explain why certain compulsive behaviors, like those seen in limerence, escalate and reinforce obsession. For instance, if the desired person occasionally engages with them, replies to messages, or likes their posts on social media, the limerent individual experiences a surge of hope and validation. Similarly, a compliment, a moment of eye contact, or a shared laugh can trigger a flood of positive emotions and reinforce the obsessive fixation.

This occasional reinforcement strengthens the compulsion to continue looking for signs of interest, as the unpredictability of the response makes each reward feel more valuable. Over time, the limerent individual becomes trapped in a cycle of seeking these small, sporadic rewards, which only deepens their emotional attachment and reinforces the obsessive fixation. The result is an escalating pattern of behavior where the limerent individual continuously seeks relief from their discomfort, only to perpetuate it further.

Intermittent reinforcement explains the enduring cycle of hope and doubt in limerence. Occasional signs of reciprocation fuel the limerent individual's belief that their feelings are mutual. This glimmer of hope keeps them emotionally invested in the pursuit of connection, even when faced with long periods of doubt and uncertainty.

The combination of fleeting hope and persistent doubt creates a self-perpetuating cycle. It can trap the limerent individual in limerence for months or years while they continue to engage in compulsive behaviors to soothe longing and maintain some sense of perceived connection and emotional reciprocation. As longing deepens, compulsive behaviors and obsessive thoughts begin to feed each other, intensifying the fixation on the desired person. Thinking becomes a way to manage overwhelming emotion, regain a sense of control, and construct imagined moments of closeness to soothe the ache. These thoughts may feel urgent and involuntary, pulling attention back to the desired other throughout the day and night. Even brief moments of stillness may quickly fill with inner dialogues, what-ifs, and imagined interactions. As these mental patterns are relied upon to regulate emotion, thinking itself can become compulsive, used not just for reflection but as a means of emotional survival. Although these thoughts may bring short-term relief, they also prolong the longing, reinforcing the attachment through repetition, imagination, and fantasy.

References

Bosworth, C. E., van Donzel, E., Lewis, B., & Pellat, C. (Eds.). (1997). *Encyclopaedia of Islam* (Vol. 4, Iran–Kha, 3rd impression). E. J. Brill. https://archive.org/details/ei2-complete

Das, G. (2018). *Kama: The riddle of desire.* Penguin Books India.

Gethin, R. (1998). *The foundations of Buddhism* (p. 121). Oxford University Press.

Harvey, P. (2013). *An introduction to Buddhism: Teachings, history and practices* (2nd ed.). Cambridge University Press.

Miller, C. M. (1993). The blazing body: Ascetic desire in Jerome's letters to Eustochium. *Journal of Early Christian Studies, 1*(1), 21–45.

Scherman, N. (1996). *Tanach: The Torah, Prophets, Writings, the twenty-four books of the Bible.* Mesorah Publications Ltd.

Skinner, B. F. (1938). *The behavior of organisms: An experimental analysis.* Appleton-Century.

Vital, C. (n.d.). *Etz Hayyim (Tree of Life), folio 11b.*

Willmott, L., & Bentley, E. (2015). Exploring the lived-experience of limerence: A journey toward authenticity. *The Qualitative Report, 20*(1), 20–38. https://doi.org/10.46743/2160-3715/2015.1420

Wyant, B. E. (2021). Treatment of limerence using a cognitive behavioral approach: A case study. *Journal of Patient Experience, 8,* 1–7. https://doi.org/10.1177/23743735211060812

6 I Can't Stop Thinking about You
Obsessive Thoughts

Thinking serves many functions. It helps us make sense of emotions and perceptions, draw conclusions, form judgments, and make decisions (Kahneman, 2011). It generates new ideas, categorizes concepts, and organizes existing knowledge. Thought also plays a key role in planning for the future, allowing scenarios to be mentally rehearsed without real-life consequences. If these scenarios are agreeable, thinking can become a source of pleasure (Klinger, 1990).

During limerence, the individual initially derives immense pleasure from thinking about the person they desire: their face, their eyes, the quality of their voice, and any positive interaction that is remembered. These thoughts bring feelings of peace, joy, bliss, soothing, and pleasure. If a limerent individual is having a hard day, they only need to think of their desired other to lift their mood. Thinking thus becomes a powerful source of stress relief, mood control, and enjoyment.

As thoughts of the desired person become repetitive, they may begin to form neural pathways and become embedded in a web of associations (Doidge, 2010). Consequently, thoughts of the desired other become more frequent, intrusive, and progressively harder to control, creating a breeding ground for obsessive thoughts that soon spiral beyond the individual's control, invading their mind throughout the day and night.

In the most intense phase, limerent thoughts become all-consuming and differ markedly from ordinary thinking. The limerent individual finds themselves constantly preoccupied with thoughts of the desired person, with the intensity of these thoughts increasing over time. At its worst, obsessive thinking can occur every minute, making it nearly impossible for the limerent individual to focus on anything else. It becomes an incessant loop of internal projections, visions, questions, and scenarios revolving around the desired other.

Thoughts of the desired person, once enjoyable and within the individual's control, quickly become intrusive and distressing. They grow frequent and invasive, entering the mind against the conscious will of the limerent individual. This shift fuels anxiety, as they can no longer glean the same pleasure from these thoughts, instead feeling distressed by their inability to control the direction of their own mind. Efforts to distract themselves or consciously

DOI: 10.4324/9781003563747-7

shift focus are usually futile. The thoughts continue to invade the limerent individual's mind, progressively seizing more and more of their psychic space.

Over time, these repeated thoughts begin to leave deeper imprints in the brain (Doidge, 2010). The more often the limerent individual thinks about the desired other, the more strongly those thought patterns are reinforced. Daily routines and environments, such as checking their phone, passing a familiar location, or sitting at their desk, can become unconsciously linked to the presence or memory of the desired other. Once these associations are in place, they may begin to trigger limerent thoughts automatically, even without intention. The thoughts do not necessarily gain emotional power, but they become more deeply wired, making them harder to resist and more likely to recur.

The time consumed by these obsessive thought loops disrupts daily functioning, making it hard to focus, complete tasks, or engage meaningfully with others. The emotional toll of these relentless thoughts brings feelings of shame, guilt, and hopelessness, as the individual feels trapped in the prison of their own mind.

The persistent thoughts of the desired other drain the limerent individual's mental energy, which, like physical energy, is finite. Only a limited amount is available each day before rest and sleep are needed to replenish focus and restore clarity (Baumeister & Tierney, 2011). The intrusive, obsessive nature of limerent thoughts siphons this limited mental energy, diverting it to sustain the limerence. This fixation traps the individual in cycles of repetitive thoughts, perpetuating and intensifying the limerent obsession.

As a result, the limerent individual has less mental energy for relationships, creative pursuits, work, and personal development. To truly grow and integrate mentally, one needs freedom to focus on their inner world, yet for the limerent individual, this inner world is hijacked by the obsession with the desired other. Their focus shifts more toward the desired person than themselves, leading to a gradual deterioration in mental health.

As limerence deepens, consciously choosing to think about the desired other may still bring moments of comfort or pleasure. But over time, these thoughts tend to surface more frequently and become increasingly difficult to control. This loss of control leads to significant distress, as the limerent individual is forced to think about the desired other far more than they wish to. The frequency and intensity of these thoughts disrupt daily life, creating feelings of being obsessed and even a sense of "going crazy." While these thoughts can still provide pleasure when intentionally engaged, it is their unwanted, automatic intrusions that cause distress.

This paradox of seeking relief through thoughts that also bring discomfort is echoed in other psychological conditions. The pattern of obsessive, unwanted thoughts in limerence shares similarities with the intrusive thinking of obsessive–compulsive disorder (OCD), where individuals are plagued by fears of germs, forgetting important details, losing items, repeatedly checking locks, or other fixations (Rachman, 2007). In both OCD and limerence, these intrusive thoughts are unwanted, repetitive, and difficult to control, leading to anxiety and a sense of mental entrapment.

Invasive and unwanted thoughts are also common in anxiety disorders, centering on worry, catastrophizing, or repetitive patterns that heighten anxiety and distress. Certain types of thoughts can activate the amygdala, triggering the body's stress response and leading to cognitive distortions that blur the line between thoughts and reality (LeDoux, 1998).

During limerence, intrusive thoughts about the desired other flood the mind. These thoughts emerge upon waking, recur throughout the day, and can be present when trying to fall asleep. The thoughts are pervasive, with the desired other even appearing in dreams, making sleep itself offer little respite. This relentless invasion of thoughts disrupts the limerent individual's natural rhythms, causing constant distraction and considerable difficulty with daily functioning.

Limerent Thoughts

Limerent thoughts are persistent, invasive, and obsessive, covering a wide range of themes and emotions, from intense desire to anxiety, sadness, and simple curiosity. At times, these thoughts take on an idealized and romantic tone, as the limerent individual attributes qualities of perfection to the desired other. They may embellish the desired person's talents and virtues, constructing an image that extends far beyond reality.

At other times, these thoughts shift toward rumination and analysis. The limerent individual meticulously dissects each remembered interaction and conversation, searching for hidden meanings or subtle clues that might validate their hopes and desires. Every word, tone, and gesture are replayed and scrutinized for signs of mutual interest or reciprocation.

Fear and worry can also dominate limerent thoughts, as the individual becomes consumed by anxiety over potential rejection or emotional unavailability. Concerns about losing affection or failing to sustain the intensity of the connection can become a major source of distress. These thoughts frequently revolve around uncertainty and self-doubt, with the limerent individual questioning their own worth in relation to the idealized desired other. The mind spirals into repetitive loops, projecting a negative self-image imagined through the desired person's eyes.

At times, limerent thoughts are emotionally neutral, driven by an obsessive curiosity about the desired other. The individual may wonder about their whereabouts, activities, and daily experiences. Even mundane details become a source of fascination, from their coffee preferences to their taste in films or music. There is a persistent, unquenchable desire to uncover every aspect of their life, as if knowing more might bring a sense of closeness or understanding.

The repetitive, obsessive nature of these thoughts becomes a barrier to effective functioning, making it difficult for the limerent individual to focus on tasks or engage fully in other areas of life. The desired other occupies their mind, eclipsing other thoughts and diverting attention from the present moment.

This intense preoccupation begins to seep into every area of the limerent individual's life. Therapy sessions may become centered entirely around thoughts and feelings about the desired person, and they often confide in any friend willing to listen. Interests unrelated to the desired other can lose their appeal, and the individual may even drift away from people who have no connection to the object of their obsession. Conversations with friends may constantly circle back to the same topic, dominated by a relentless need to discuss and analyze every detail of their infatuation.

The limerent individual may become isolated or rely heavily on a few trusted friends for emotional support, validation, and understanding, drawing them into the ongoing analysis of the desired person. Over time, these conversations extend well beyond the usual boundaries of emotional processing and begin to drain the friendships. Those unfamiliar with the intrusive and uncontrollable nature of limerence may become frustrated, as the constant focus on the desired person can feel overwhelming, excessive, or self-absorbed. Eventually, this can strain relationships and test the patience of even the most supportive friends. Despite providing support and validation, these conversations cannot resolve the obsessive nature of limerent thoughts. Friends may begin to recognize the unhealthy toll of the fixation, leading to misunderstandings, unhelpful advice, or gradual withdrawal. This dynamic may leave the limerent individual isolated once again, alone with their obsessive, invasive thoughts.

In therapy, limerent individuals measure their progress by small accomplishments, such as "I thought about them less today," or "they weren't my first thought upon waking today, for the first time in months." These markers highlight both the intensity and intrusiveness of limerent thoughts, as well as the ongoing struggle to regain control of their mind.

Triggers

Triggers play a significant role in sparking obsessive thought loops during limerence. Although a specific trigger isn't required for thoughts of the desired person to arise, certain experiences can amplify these obsessive patterns. Meeting with the desired other, passive online interactions with them, seeing or speaking to someone connected to them, visiting familiar places they frequent, or even hearing a song associated with them can all trigger a cascade of thoughts.

Messages, emails, phone calls, or any form of communication from the desired other can unleash torrents of obsessive thoughts. After any direct contact, the limerent individual may spend hours, days, or even weeks dissecting the interaction from every possible angle.

Social media adds another dimension to these challenges. Any activity from the desired person on social media can instantly spark obsessive thoughts, fueling the limerent individual's imagination and triggering intense rumination. Discovering shared interests or hobbies can intensify the infatuation, while any insight into the desired person's personal life may stir a sense of longing and a yearning for deeper connection.

The desired person's significant life updates, such as a new job, relocation, or relationship status change, can act as potent triggers for obsessive thought loops. These updates may lead the limerent individual into hours of mental dissection, attempting to interpret the meaning and implications of each change.

Any new information about the desired other is intricately analyzed and woven into a complex web of connections that fuels the limerent individual's fascination. These obsessive, invasive thoughts consume hours of mental energy, pulling focus from the individual's actual life, intensifying longing, and perpetuating limerence.

Obsessive Thoughts as Control

The desire for control is deeply rooted in human nature. Throughout evolution, having control likely increased survival by helping individuals anticipate and avoid potential threats (Rothbaum et al., 1982). As a result, people feel more at ease when they can exert some level of control, while situations that lie beyond their influence tend to provoke anxiety and distress. For this reason, obsessive thoughts may be viewed as an unconscious attempt to impose order on perceived chaos (Salkovskis et al., 1995). The repetitive mental loop, while unproductive, can feel stabilizing simply because it is familiar.

These patterns may also reflect emotional dynamics shaped by early attachment experiences, particularly in a childhood marked by chaos, inconsistency, or emotional unpredictability. When core needs for safety, attunement, or stability go unmet, they give rise to lasting emotional preoccupations in adulthood. In such cases, obsessive thought loops may serve as an unhealthy yet familiar anchor, offering an illusory sense of control or stability in a world that otherwise feels chaotic and unstable.

While further research is needed to fully understand the link between childhood experiences, attachment dynamics, and obsessive thought patterns, some studies offer support for this connection. For example, individuals with histories of emotional neglect or inconsistent caregiving may develop heightened attachment anxiety in adulthood, which can contribute to obsessive-compulsive tendencies (Hodny et al., 2022). These tendencies manifest as repetitive thoughts and behaviors aimed at managing anxiety and creating a sense of control, reflecting deeper attachment-related fears and unmet emotional needs.

These underlying emotional patterns can be easily misunderstood by others, leading to misguided responses to the distress caused by limerence. Friends, and even well-meaning therapists who are unfamiliar with its complexity, may advise the individual to just "let it go" or "focus on something else". Although such suggestions come from a place of care, they tend to oversimplify the psychological dynamics involved.

To find relief, the limerent individual may try to follow this advice. They attempt to repress their thoughts, telling themselves to move on and stop thinking about the desired person. This repression usually intensifies the obsessive loop, amplifying the very thoughts they are trying so hard to suppress.

Rebound Effect

The psychological phenomenon known as the "rebound effect" sheds light on this paradoxical response to repression. When an individual actively tries to suppress or avoid certain thoughts or emotions, the mind tends to bounce back with greater force, bringing those exact thoughts and emotions to the forefront of consciousness (Wegner, 1994). This effect is explained by the theory of *ironic processes*, which suggests that attempts at mental control engage two processes: an operating process that searches for desired mental content and a monitoring process that scans for the unwanted content.

Under normal conditions, the operating process dominates, helping an individual stay focused on preferred thoughts. But when cognitive capacity is reduced due to stress, fatigue, or intense emotional distress—as during limerence—the monitoring process can take over, making the individual more sensitive to the very thoughts they wish to avoid (Wegner, 1994). It is like trying to push a beach ball underwater: No matter how hard one tries to hold it down; it eventually resurfaces with even more vigor. As the saying goes, "what we resist persists." When a person is distressed and engages in a battle of resistance with their own thoughts and emotions, they inadvertently give those thoughts more power and attention. This creates a frustrating cycle where the harder a limerent individual tries to suppress the thoughts of the desired other, the more they find themselves consumed by them.

The effort to repress thoughts also demands constant mental energy and vigilance, which only deepens the obsession. As the limerent individual becomes more mentally fatigued and distressed, their attention fixates on *not* thinking about the person, ironically making thoughts of them more central. In essence, the very act of trying to repress thoughts of the desired other serves as a continual reminder of them, further fueling the obsession and perpetuating the cycle of limerence. Further, when one attempts to repress certain thoughts, those thoughts may resurface in unexpected forms, catching the person off guard. The mind, in its persistent drive to express and process internal experience, seeks alternative outlets for what is being pushed out of conscious awareness (Jung, 1992).

Limerent Dreams

During limerence, the obsessive thoughts that consume the individual's waking hours can also infiltrate their dreams. It is not uncommon for limerent individuals to dream about the desired person, even in the absence of recent interaction. The constancy of obsessive thoughts throughout the day may contribute to the frequency and intensity of these dreams, as the subconscious mind attempts to process unresolved emotions and unfulfilled desires (Jung, 1992).

Dreams can be understood as visual projections of the subconscious, processing and integrating both internal experience and waking preoccupations. For the limerent individual, dreams involving the desired other may create a heightened sense of spiritual connection, reinforcing the belief that the bond transcends the physical realm. These dreams can deepen the perception of a destined or profound connection, strengthening the obsession and fostering a sense of union or reciprocation that feels real within the dream experience. As a result, the dreams not only reflect the preoccupation but also fuel it, magnifying the obsession and deepening the emotional entanglement.

The link between obsessive thoughts and dreams in limerence offers a fascinating glimpse into the subconscious mind. Dreams may reveal insights into the limerent individual's deepest desires, fears, and unmet emotional needs, providing a unique window into the complexities of the psyche and illuminating the underlying psychological processes at play. Just as dreams offer glimpses into the subconscious, fantasy and daydreams serve as a conscious playground for the mind to explore its desires and yearnings.

References

Baumeister, R. F., & Tierney, J. (2011). *Willpower: Rediscovering the greatest human strength.* Penguin Press.

Doidge, N. (2010). *The brain that changes itself: Stories of personal triumph from the frontiers of brain science.* Scribe Publications.

Hodny, F., Ociskova, M., Prasko, J., Vanek, J., Visnovsky, J., Sollar, T., Slepecky, M., Nesnídal, V., & Kolek, A. (2022). Early life experiences and adult attachment in obsessive-compulsive disorder: Part 2: Therapeutic effectiveness of combined cognitive behavioural therapy and pharmacotherapy in treatment-resistant inpatients. *Neuroendocrinology Letters, 43*(6), 345–358.

Jung, C. G. (1992). *Dreams.* Princeton University Press.

Kahneman, D. (2011). *Thinking, fast and slow* (eBook ed.). Penguin Books Limited.

Klinger, E. (1990). *Daydreaming: Using waking fantasy and imagery for self-knowledge and creativity.* J.P. Tarcher.

LeDoux, J. E. (1998). *The emotional brain: The mysterious underpinnings of emotional life.* Simon & Schuster.

Rachman, S. (2007). Unwanted intrusive images in obsessive compulsive disorders. *Journal of Behavior Therapy and Experimental Psychiatry, 38*(4), 402–410. https://doi.org/10.1016/j.jbtep.2007.10.008

Rothbaum, F., Weisz, J. R., & Snyder, S. S. (1982). Changing the world and changing the self: A two-process model of perceived control. *Journal of Personality and Social Psychology, 42*(1), 5–37. https://doi.org/10.1037/0022-3514.42.1.5

Salkovskis, P. M., Richards, H. C., & Forrester, E. (1995). The relationship between obsessional problems and intrusive thoughts. *Behavioural and Cognitive Psychotherapy, 23*(3), 281–299. https://doi.org/10.1017/S1352465800015885

Wegner, D. M. (1994). Ironic processes of mental control. *Psychological Review, 101*(1), 34–52. https://doi.org/10.1037/0033-295X.101.1.34

7 The Things I'd Like to Do with You

Daydreaming and Fantasy

Adaptive Fantasy

Fantasy and daydreams play an important role in human consciousness. One might assume that from an evolutionary perspective, these mental processes would hinder survival, as it could seem more advantageous to remain focused and alert to potential threats. But this is not the case. The human brain is wired for fantasy and daydreaming, and these processes offer significant benefits to overall wellbeing. Research shows that the brain activates a specific network, known as the *default mode network*, during internally focused states such as daydreaming and imaginative thinking about the self, others, the past, and the future. This network, which is particularly active during restful or non-task-oriented states, supports reflection, the simulation of future scenarios, and the integration of personal experience (Menon, 2023).

Fantasy and daydreaming may serve as cognitive simulations and planning mechanisms. Through mental rehearsal of future scenarios, individuals enhance their ability to anticipate challenges, devise strategies, and make adaptive decisions (Menon, 2023). This capacity for simulation and planning may have advantages in terms of survival, resource acquisition, and navigating social interactions. By mentally exploring different possibilities and outcomes, individuals better prepare for future events, increasing their chances of life success.

Mind-wandering has also been associated with enhanced creativity, as it enables free association: the automatic tendency to create links and associations between concepts (Sun et al., 2021). By engaging in imaginative processes, individuals can generate new and innovative ideas, think beyond conventional boundaries, and discover novel solutions to challenges (Zedelius & Schooler, 2016).

Throughout human history, great innovations, discoveries, and theories have emerged from allowing the mind to wander. Legend has it that Isaac Newton formulated gravitational theory after dreamily watching an apple drop from a tree. Einstein's theory of relativity is said to have stemmed from his daydream of riding alongside a beam of light. Nikola Tesla reported that his inventions appeared to him in visions during daydreaming, and Henri

DOI: 10.4324/9781003563747-8

Poincaré attributed several of his mathematical and geometrical discoveries to imaginative processes.

Discoveries, ideas, and innovations that arise through fantasy and daydreams are the result of a process known as *incubation* (Wallas, 2014). During incubation, the mind continues to process information about a particular problem or puzzle in the background. The subconscious sifts through possibilities and makes new creative connections during daydreaming. After this process of incubation, a breakthrough can occur. When the individual takes a break from active work, the creative unconscious takes over, allowing new concepts to be accessed consciously. Artists, writers, philosophers, mathematicians, psychologists, and others have all reported these kinds of "aha" moments after periods of daydreaming and mind-wandering. Incubation draws on the subconscious, which is active during daydreams and fantasy, to enhance creativity and bring new ideas to the surface.

Fantasy and daydreaming may also provide valuable opportunities for emotional clarity and regulation (Shiota & Nomura, 2022). Through imagined scenarios and different perspectives, individuals can distance themselves from immediate stressors, gaining insight into their emotions and a renewed sense of control. This reflective space allows the mind to explore and process complex emotions, reducing reactivity and supporting wellbeing.

Fantasy and daydreaming may also serve an adaptive function by promoting social and emotional bonding. Imagining scenarios or narrative worlds helps individuals explore their beliefs about themselves and others (Dill-Shackleford et al., 2016). By visualizing meaningful social connections, people can strengthen personal bonds and develop empathy, which supports both emotional resilience and social cohesion.

Despite the many advantages, there can also be a darker side to fantasy and daydreaming. While these processes can inspire creativity and insight, they may also serve as a means of escape or dissociation, especially when they become habitual. Some studies suggest that excessive mind-wandering is linked to decreased happiness (Killingsworth & Gilbert, 2010).

In the case of limerence, fantasy and daydreams take on an intensified role, consuming substantial time and mental energy. For limerent individuals, these fantasies and daydreams revolve entirely around the desired person and can lead them to withdraw from real social interactions in favor of solitary immersion in imagined scenarios.

Limerent Fantasy

During limerence, the content of fantasies deviates markedly from the type of creative and productive daydreaming that might explore philosophical, mathematical, or artistic ideas. Rather than channeling mental energy into problem-solving, innovation, or the generation of new ideas, even the subconscious mind becomes narrowly focused on the desired other. The hijack of the mind is thus complete: Limerence not only overtakes conscious thought but also seizes control of the subconscious. Limerence enlists the default mode network, redirecting it entirely toward fantasies about the desired person. As a result, the mental resources usually reserved for personal growth, rest, integration, and creativity are fully diverted toward maintaining the obsessive loop, depriving the individual of the cognitive and emotional benefits normally gained from healthy, integrative daydreaming.

The limerent individual may spend hours immersed in elaborate fantasies centered on the desired other. These imagined scenarios create a sense of illusory intimacy and emotional connection. Their content can vary widely, ranging from intensely erotic to mundane, everyday moments.

In these imagined encounters, the limerent individual engages in conversations and experiences with the desired other that seem to fulfil their deepest longings. This immersive fantasy world provides a temporary respite from longing, yet ultimately reinforces the intensity of the infatuation, as each imagined moment of union strengthens the emotional hold of their idealized connection.

The tendency to fantasize about the desired person may begin innocuously, as an occasional pleasure the limerent individual engages in. It might start as a simple, harmless desire to think about the desired other and relish a sense of connection within the realm of imagination. As limerence intensifies though, these fantasies begin to take on a life of their own, demanding more and more time, attention, and energy. They can consume hours on end, distracting the limerent individual from other important aspects of life and impairing their ability to function effectively.

The pleasure derived from daydreaming and fantasy reinforces the pattern. Each time the limerent individual immerses themselves in these gratifying inner worlds, they receive an emotional reward: the illusion of closeness with the desired other. Over time, this may strengthen the neural pathways linked to their desires (Doidge, 2010). With repeated indulgence, the fantasies grow more vivid and deeply ingrained, tightening limerence's grip on their psyche. The result is a self-reinforcing loop, fueling the need for more fantasy and further intensifying the obsession.

Realistic and Idealized Fantasies

The allure of limerent fantasies stems from their capacity to evoke a vivid, though illusory, sense of connection and fulfillment. Within this fantasy world, the limerent individual constructs two main types of scenarios: *realistic* and *idealized* fantasies.

Realistic fantasies are rooted in actual experiences and interactions with the desired other, involving reliving past moments, replaying past conversations, and envisioning future encounters that align with the limerent individual's perception of reality. Although based on real-life experiences, these fantasies are elevated by heightened emotions and wishful thinking. The limerent individual may romanticize even neutral interactions, attributing deep meaning to them and amplifying their significance.

Idealized fantasies, on the other hand, go beyond the bounds of reality. Here, the limerent individual creates an imagined, perfect version of the desired other, projecting their own desires, needs, and ideals onto them. This fantasy version embodies qualities and behaviors that align with the limerent individual's deepest longings and unmet emotional needs. The desired person becomes an embodiment of an ideal partner or soulmate, someone seemingly flawless and uniquely suited to fulfil all the limerent individual's desires, creating a "halo effect" where the desired person is placed in an unreachable realm of perfection.

Realistic and idealized fantasies may serve distinct purposes in limerence. Realistic fantasies may offer emotional validation and reinforcement, as they are grounded in actual experiences and interactions. These fantasies allow the limerent individual to relive moments of perceived connection and intimacy, providing temporary relief from the discomfort of longing. Idealized fantasies may provide an escape from the disappointments and unpredictability of life or real relationships, allowing the limerent individual to experience the illusion of the idealized connection that they crave without the complexities, risks, or consequences that may exist in reality.

Themes of Limerent Fantasy

Themes of limerent fantasy cut across both realistic and idealized scenarios, with erotic fantasies being among the most intense and consuming. These fantasies may be rooted in real memories of past sexual experiences with the desired other but, even when grounded in reality, they are typically heightened by emotions, longing, and idealization. Others are entirely imagined, having no basis in real-life interaction, yet they can feel equally vivid, compelling, and emotionally affecting.

Erotic fantasies during limerence can reawaken the individual's sexuality, particularly if it has been dormant, stirring desires with newfound intensity. Even for those already in touch with their sexuality, these fantasies can become a potent and continuous source of arousal. The combination of emotional longing and sexual stimulation creates a powerful internal loop that may easily become compulsive.

Over time, the brain may begin to associate sexual arousal with the desired other (Doidge, 2010). Through repeated pairing of erotic thought and physical pleasure, the image or idea of the desired other can become central to the limerent individual's sexual experience. Eventually, these associations may arise automatically during arousal and become a prerequisite for orgasm, whether alone or with a partner.

This reinforcement loop can deepen the emotional and psychological attachment to the desired other. The limerent individual may come to feel that their desire, pleasure, and even their capacity for intimacy is tied directly to this one person. In some cases, the fantasy becomes more emotionally significant than any real interaction. This blurs the line between imagined union and actual connection and contributes to the deep sense of emotional or even spiritual attachment to the desired other. The result is an even stronger limerent bond and an increased difficulty in breaking free from the obsession.

Another common type of fantasy in limerence involves emotional union, where the desired other is imagined offering love, care, and emotional reciprocation. These fantasies may be grounded in real interactions, such as moments of deep eye contact, words of affirmation, physical affection, or past expressions of reassurance and commitment, which are replayed and sometimes embellished in the mind. In other cases, they are entirely idealized, with no actual basis, yet still carry the same emotional weight. The desired other might be imagined saying "I love you," proposing marriage, raising a family together, or participating in meaningful rituals that symbolize emotional depth and commitment.

These fantasies may momentarily soothe the ache of unfulfilled longing by creating the illusion that the feelings are mutual. Even though imagined, the emotional satisfaction they provide can be profound. For the limerent individual, these scenarios may enhance the felt sense of intimacy and connection with the desired other, reinforcing the emotional attachment and deepening the bond.

In some cases, the limerent individual may come to believe that these emotional or sexual fantasies are somehow sensed or shared by the desired other. This belief in a telepathic or energetic connection can add a powerful layer of perceived intimacy. The limerent individual may feel that the desired person is aware of or even responding to their inner world, whether through sexual energy, emotional union, or even mundane mental imagery. This experience can form its own kind of fantasy, shaped by the belief in a psychic or intuitive connection.

Other limerent fantasies may be completely neutral in nature, focusing not on romance or sexuality, but on ordinary moments involving the desired other. These might include imagining them at work, drinking tea, cooking, buttoning a shirt, or walking through a room. The limerent individual may also picture themselves carrying out everyday acts of care, like making breakfast for the desired other, massaging their shoulders, or tending to them when they're sick. Some of these fantasies may draw on real memories, while others are entirely imagined.

Even though they lack overt emotional or erotic content, these neutral fantasies can still deepen the sense of closeness. They allow the limerent individual to mentally inhabit the everyday life of the desired other, creating an illusion of familiarity and shared experience. In this way, even mundane imagery becomes meaningful, further intensifying the emotional bond and sustaining the sense of connection in the absence of real or satisfying relational contact.

Impacts of Limerent Fantasy

Continued indulgence in both realistic and idealized fantasies can distort the limerent individual's perception of reality. The more time they spend in the fantasy realm, the more distant and unreal the actual world may begin to feel. This immersion can also distort their perception of the desired other. They may become detached from the real nuances and complexities of the person's character and motivations, projecting an idealized version instead. As a result, genuine emotional connection becomes harder to achieve, not only with the desired other but also with others in their life as well.

The contrast between the fantasy world and reality can also give rise to cognitive dissonance. The limerent individual may feel torn between blissful, emotionally gratifying fantasies and the harsh reality of the unattainability of their idealized desires. This dissonance leads to emotional distress, reinforcing their obsession and preoccupation with the desired person. Inner conflicts emerge as they oscillate between the comforting allure of imagination and the painful awareness that their fantasies remain unfulfilled. This emotional turbulence creates a profound sense of turmoil and instability as the individual grapples with the conflicting emotions of limerence.

Limerent fantasies can also significantly impact self-esteem and self-perception. As the individual becomes increasingly absorbed in these fantasies, they may develop an idealized self-image in relation to the desired person, seeing themselves as more desirable, worthy, or lovable within the confines of their imaginative world. This idealized self-image may then be shattered when they confront the reality that the desired person remains out of reach. This dissonance can lead to feelings of inadequacy, unworthiness, or rejection, negatively affecting mental health.

The emotional consequences of limerent fantasies can be far-reaching, infiltrating many aspects of an individual's life. They may struggle to maintain emotional balance, as their feelings become closely tied to the ebb and flow of their fantasies. The intense investment in the imagined connection can foster a sense of dependency and obsession, making it difficult to find emotional stability outside the fantasy world.

As the limerent individual immerses themselves deeper in their imaginative world, the line between fantasy and reality begins to blur. The once-clear boundaries between these realms become increasingly hazy, making it difficult to distinguish what is real from what is purely imagined. They may find themselves yearning for the fantasy world, craving a connection that exists only in their mind.

This detachment from reality can have profound effects on their emotional wellbeing. The intense longing for a fictionalized version of the desired other can lead to dissatisfaction and discontentment with real relationships and connections in their life. Establishing and maintaining authentic connections becomes challenging, as they continuously compare real-life experiences to the fantasy they have created in their mind.

Fantasies play a significant role in maintaining the limerent state, as they perpetuate the attachment and intensify the longing felt by the individual. Within this imaginative realm, the limerent individual can nurture and sustain their emotional connection to the desired person. By continually engaging in vivid mental narratives, they reinforce the emotional bond and deepen their attachment, further entrenching themselves in the grip of limerence.

Functions of Limerent Fantasy

Fantasies can serve as a form of escapism and avoidance, offering an alternative world where the limerent individual can find solace and comfort. These imagined spaces shield them from the complexities and disappointments of real-life interactions. By immersing themselves in fantasy, they can temporarily disconnect from daily challenges and uncertainty, finding relief in the illusory realm created within the mind.

This kind of escapism may have roots in early childhood experiences, where dissociation or emotional numbing develops to cope with neglect or trauma (van der Kolk, 2015). For some, fantasy becomes a protective strategy for managing emotional pain. In adulthood, especially during periods of intense, unresolved longing, these early coping patterns may reemerge. Within the limerent state, fantasy becomes a familiar refuge, deepening the attachment and reinforcing emotional dependence on the imagined connection.

Reliance on fantasies as a coping mechanism can perpetuate the limerent state and impede the individual's progress toward emotional resolution. The more they indulge in these fantasies, the deeper the attachment becomes, making it increasingly difficult to break free from the cycle of longing. These fantasies provide a steady source of emotional gratification, reinforcing the belief that the desired person holds the key to their happiness and fulfillment.

Additionally, limerent fantasies offer the individual an illusion of control in an otherwise unpredictable and uncertain situation. Within these imagined scenarios, they can shape and manipulate the responses, actions, and emotions of the desired person, granting a temporary sense of agency and power over their imagined relationship. This illusion of control may feel comforting and empowering, further strengthening the attachment and fueling their desire.

Dysfunction of Limerent Fantasy

While fantasy may begin as a soothing refuge, its repeated use can gradually shift from adaptive to limiting. What starts as a coping mechanism to regulate emotional distress can become a mental habit that displaces engagement with real-life experiences. The fantasy may offer comfort, but it also distances the individual from opportunities for genuine connection, personal growth, and emotional integration. As the inner world becomes more compelling than the outer one, the line between soothing and self-sabotaging begins to blur.

During limerence, fantasy and daydreaming can become restrictive rather than liberating. The dream state that should encourage growth and integration instead strengthens the obsessive loop, narrowing focus onto the imagined connection with the desired other. Rather than facilitating self-discovery or personal fulfillment, limerent fantasy further traps the individual in a cycle of longing and fixation, redirecting mental energy away from constructive pursuits. Here, the healing potential of fantasy is inverted, transforming into a mechanism that reinforces an idealized attachment to the desired person and limits genuine emotional engagement with the world.

When the limerent individual inevitably awakens from their fantasy world, they may find reality even more barren than they remember leaving it, leading to profound pain and disorientation. In this sense, it is not the fantasy itself that causes suffering, but the painful return to a reality that feels hollow by comparison.

References

Dill-Shackleford, K. E., Vinney, C., & Hopper-Losenicky, K. (2016). Connecting the dots between fantasy and reality: The social psychology of our engagement with fictional narrative and its functional value. *Social and Personality Psychology Compass, 10*(11), 634–646. https://doi.org/10.1111/spc3.12274

Doidge, N. (2010). *The brain that changes itself: Stories of personal triumph from the frontiers of brain science*. Scribe Publications.

Killingsworth, M. A., & Gilbert, D. T. (2010). A wandering mind is an unhappy mind. *Science, 330*(6006), 932. https://doi.org/10.1126/science.1192439

Menon, V. (2023). 20 years of the default mode network: A review and synthesis. *Neuron, 111*(16), 2469–2487. https://doi.org/10.1016/j.neuron.2023.04.023

Shiota, S., & Nomura, M. (2022). Role of fantasy in emotional clarity and emotional regulation in empathy: A preliminary study. *Frontiers in Psychology, 13*, 912165. https://doi.org/10.3389/fpsyg.2022.912165

Sun, J., He, L., Chen, Q., Yang, W., Wei, D., & Qiu, J. (2021). The bright side and dark side of daydreaming predict creativity together through brain functional connectivity. *Human Brain Mapping, 43*(3), 902–914. https://doi.org/10.1002/hbm.25693

van der Kolk, B. A. (2015). *The body keeps the score: Mind, brain and body in the transformation of trauma* (1st ed.). Penguin Books.

Wallas, G. (2014). *The art of thought*. Solis Press. (Original work published 1926).

Zedelius, C. M., & Schooler, J. W. (2016). The richness of inner experience: Relating styles of daydreaming to creative processes. *Frontiers in Psychology, 6*, 2063. https://doi.org/10.3389/fpsyg.2015.02063

8   Tell Me You Love Me
Mutual, Unexpressed, and Unrequited Limerence

Judging by popular discourse, there is a common misconception that limerence is always one-sided and unrequited. In reality, limerence can manifest in different relational dynamics. *Mutual limerence* occurs when two individuals experience limerence for each other but external circumstances, such as timing, distance, or existing relationships prevent them from being together. *Unexpressed limerence* happens when the limerent individual does not disclose their feelings and therefore remains unsure whether the other person feels the same. *Unrequited limerence* is when it is clear to the limerent individual that their feelings are not returned.

Mutual Limerence

Mutual limerence occurs when two individuals experience an intense and obsessive preoccupation with each other. Both have intrusive thoughts, vivid fantasies, and an overwhelming longing to be together. In most cases, barriers or obstacles prevent the pair from fully realizing their connection, even when they are aware of their shared feelings. The intensity of limerence can motivate some individuals to take significant steps to overcome these obstacles and pursue a relationship. If these barriers are resolved and the uncertainty fades, limerence dissipates, leaving space for the development of a more stable and enduring relationship that is grounded in reality.

As doubt diminishes and the relationship becomes tangible, the balance that sustains limerence is disrupted. Obsessive thoughts and fantasies are gradually replaced by a grounded and realistic perception of the other person. This shift allows the relationship to move beyond idealization, offering an opportunity for love, security, and genuine connection to develop.

During this transition, the idealization of the other person gives way to a deeper understanding of their complexities, including both strengths and flaws. This evolution can test the relationship. Some individuals may become disillusioned when faced with the reality of the person they once idealized, leading to the relationship's end. Others may find that their connection deepens, enabling them to form a stable and fulfilling bond rooted in mutual understanding and shared commitment.

DOI: 10.4324/9781003563747-9

Case Study: Eleanor

I was married to Gregory when I first met Jacob at a social evening. He was a friend of Gregory's. Gregory and I had two children, and Jacob and his wife Leah had three. When I first met Jacob, I took an immediate dislike to him. He seemed pompous and looked ridiculous in knee-high Scottish Highland socks while sporting an affected English Oxford accent. Other than that, I was hardly aware of him. To this day, I still don't know when or why my attitude began to change, eventually growing into an all-consuming obsession.

It began as a kind of curiosity that fed upon itself, becoming more daring and compelling with each step. First, there were exchanged glances, then touching, then conspiring to meet, and finally, an uncontrollable ecstasy that exploded into an affair lasting for years.

Eventually, in an attempt to end our affair, Jacob left the country with his wife and children. During this time, we mostly didn't speak, but toward the end we did, and we both realized we were still not over it. After three years of trying to stay apart, we gave up. Apart from the hopelessness of ever ending the obsession between us, our children were now old enough for us to explain why their lives were about to change so dramatically.

Jacob came back, and we resumed our affair. He wanted us to leave our marriages and be together. I wasn't sure. I enjoyed the exhilaration of the affair and feared that settling into a normal life together would extinguish the passion we shared. Eventually, we did get together, and Jacob and I lived in what became a truly passionate, intimate, and loving relationship for the next 29 years, until his death in 1994. My children loved him. After his death I never remarried. He is the love of my life.

This case illustrates a scenario of mutual limerence that ultimately resolved through the formation of a real, tangible, and secure relationship. The story concludes with the dissolution of limerence and the creation of a happy, enduring partnership that lasted until the death of one partner.

However, limerence does not always resolve through the formation of a tangible relationship. Sometimes, mutual limerence exists between two individuals, but they choose not to break the boundaries or overcome the obstacles preventing them from moving beyond their limerent state. This may be because they wish to avoid causing pain to others, because they genuinely love their spouses and are committed to resisting feelings of limerence they do not want to act on, or because they feel unable or unwilling to cross cultural or familial barriers.

In such cases, limerent individuals find themselves caught in a painful paradox. On the one hand, they experience the exhilaration and euphoria of having their feelings reciprocated by the person they desire. On the other hand, external barriers or their own conflicting wishes for their lives prevent a union, casting doubt and uncertainty on the possibility of achieving the connection they long for. This creates a complex emotional experience, as both limerent individuals grapple with the conflicting emotions of joy and hope on one side, and doubt and longing on the other. These barriers create ambivalence and leave both individuals in a state of limbo, unable to fully let go of or embrace the relationship they desire.

The presence of external obstacles in cases of mutual limerence intensifies longing and prolongs the cycle of obsessive thoughts, fantasies, and emotional turmoil. The limerent individual oscillates between hope and despair, their emotions heightened by the knowledge that the person they desire shares their feelings. While this reciprocation may offer comfort, it also amplifies their torment as they confront the painful reality that being together seems impossible.

This challenging dynamic can prolong the duration of limerence, sustaining the intense emotional attachment and making it difficult for the individuals to move forward. In this way, mutual limerence becomes a bittersweet experience, a constant reminder of what could be but remains unattainable. The limerent individuals may cling to the fantasy of union and continue to seek soothing through signs of reciprocation. Meanwhile, as time slips away, they miss opportunities to fully engage with their present reality.

The internal struggle between desire and reality creates a deep emotional tension, making it difficult for the limerent individuals to find closure and move forward. Navigating mutual limerence amid external barriers demands careful emotional management, difficult decision-making, and the pursuit of acceptance of unfulfilled longing. The limerent individuals must confront their desires, weigh the potential consequences of their actions, and consider the broader impact on everyone involved.

This journey requires self-reflection, resilience, and a willingness to face the complexities of love and relationships. It compels the limerent individuals to look inward, exploring their motivations, fears, and hopes. They must reconcile themselves with the reality that their deepest longings may be obstructed by external circumstances beyond their control.

In navigating mutual limerence amid external barriers, the limerent individuals confront the complex interplay of desire, emotional dependence, and the external forces that shape their reality. This experience highlights the profound impact of limerence, and the significant challenges faced when external circumstances obstruct the fulfillment of deeply held desires.

Case Study: Lily

There is a guy who I have known for a long time. He is a little bit older than me, and we have always had a peripheral presence in each other's lives, but he never really paid much attention to me until I grew up.

Then, we had an intimate encounter, and it felt very good. Over the next few years, we did this several times, but always in secret, and we never discussed what it meant or defined our relationship in any way. I had strong feelings for him, but I didn't tell him out of fear of rejection. We both kept dating other people.

After that, we didn't talk for a long time, many years passed, and both of us entered into serious relationships.

Then one day, I saw him again, and after a bit of casual small talk, I found myself silently staring into his eyes, and all my old feelings resurfaced. I opened up to him about my past feelings and some lingering emotions. I thought he would deflect the conversation, as it was quite inappropriate, but to my surprise (and delight), he revealed that he had similar feelings toward me and that memories of our past encounters still crossed his mind. We talked a little about our history and why things never worked out between us. I left feeling closer to him than ever.

After that, we exchanged a few texts and met up once or twice, under the pretext of "discussing our feelings," but really, I think we just wanted to see each other again. These encounters were in secret, once again, slipping easily back into the old dynamic.

Then I became obsessed with him. I couldn't stop thinking about him, wanting him, and reminiscing. Thoughts, fantasies, memories, and communication with him consumed me. It was confusing and distracting. I thought about him constantly and longed for him deeply. I tried to stop, but I couldn't. During that time, we continued talking and essentially deepened our emotional connection. We exchanged secret love messages and met discreetly a couple of times.

My longing and desire for him grew stronger, and although I was unsure about his feelings at first, it eventually became clear that they were mutual. We were completely captivated by each other, but we couldn't be together. He wasn't even allowed to talk to me as his partner became suspicious. We tried to stop communicating, but we couldn't.

It got more intense over a few years, and then eventually his partner found out we'd been talking, so we stopped. The obsession completely threw me. I had never felt so out of control in my entire life. The consequences were messy and painful, and it stirred up so much past trauma and old wounds for me. It was, honestly, a massive headfuck that I still don't fully understand.

Unexpressed Limerence

In some situations, a person experiencing limerence may encounter significant challenges that prevent them from expressing their feelings to the person they desire. The fear of rejection or embarrassment can act as a powerful deterrent, making disclosure seem too risky. Additionally, situations where confessing feelings might be deemed inappropriate, such as when the desired person is a colleague, a student, or someone connected to their existing relationships, add further complexity. These barriers can prevent the limerent individual from seeking clarity or closure, leaving their feelings unaddressed and unexpressed.

Unexpressed limerence perpetuates uncertainty and internal turmoil. The inability to communicate their emotions leaves the limerent individual without a clear response, perpetuating the cycle of obsessive thoughts and fantasies. This lack of resolution creates a psychological limbo where the individual remains trapped between longing for reciprocation and the painful reality of unfulfilled desire. Without the opportunity to openly convey their emotions, the limerent individual is unable to resolve their feelings or move forward.

This situation poses profound emotional challenges. The absence of expression and closure prevents the limerent individual from exploring the possibilities of reciprocation or rejection, and leaves them unable to gain insights into the desired person's thoughts and feelings. This uncertainty intensifies the internal struggle between desire and reality, as the limerent individual grapples with the weight of unexpressed emotions. The prolonged uncertainty can sustain their limerence indefinitely, as the lack of closure allows their imagination to fill the void with "what-ifs" and fantasies.

In cultural discourse, people who disclose their feelings in ethically fraught situations can be judged harshly, particularly when the desired person is already in a relationship. However, this judgment frequently overlooks the reality of limerence as a deeply distressing and obsessive experience over which the individual has little control. Disclosure in these cases, while fraught with complexity, can be seen as a form of self-preservation. It may provide relief from the immense psychological burden of unexpressed limerence, offering the limerent individual a chance to reclaim their emotional wellbeing. Understanding this perspective invites a more empathetic view, as disclosure might not be only about pursuing reciprocation but also about escaping the relentless torment of unexpressed desire.

The prolonged duration of unexpressed limerence presents further challenges, extending over months or years. During this time, the limerent individual remains emotionally invested in a connection that exists purely in their imagination. This is emotionally draining and psychologically taxing.

The toll of unexpressed limerence manifests in various ways, including emotional instability, as the individual oscillates between hope and disappointment. The persistent unfulfilled desire can lead to anxiety and depression, further exacerbating their distress. Over time, the undisclosed nature of their feelings may also impact their self-esteem, causing them to question their worth and desirability. The limerent individual remains caught in an exhausting cycle of yearning and uncertainty, struggling to reconcile their inner turmoil with the reality of their situation.

Case Study: Amelia

I first realized I was drawn to Dr Carter during the second semester of my philosophy degree. At first, it felt like nothing more than admiration. He was brilliant, articulate, and had a way of making even the driest material seem fascinating. I've always admired people who are smart, so I didn't think much of it. But as the weeks went on, I noticed myself looking forward to his lectures more than any other class. I started sitting near the front, hoping he'd notice me, and my heart would race whenever he spoke.

It wasn't long before I realized this was more than just admiration. I couldn't stop thinking about him. I started wondering what kind of person he was outside of uni. What made him happy? What kind of people did he admire or find attractive? What did he think about when he was alone? Did he have hidden fears or secrets he never shared? I found myself daydreaming about scenarios where we'd connect, imagining conversations where he'd open up to me. I knew I couldn't say anything, but it was so hard not to.

I thought about him all the time. Being in his class felt intoxicating, like I was high, and I couldn't concentrate on anything but him and wondering if he felt the same about me. I started analyzing how he acted toward me.

I began searching for him online, finding his faculty bio and staring at his photo for far longer than I wanted to admit. I had never acted this way about anyone before. It was strange, and I felt ashamed as I was doing it, but I couldn't stop. When he made references to his family it stung me, but I still wanted to know more. I wanted to know everything about him, even if it made me feel worse. It felt like trying to solve a puzzle with missing pieces, and I couldn't walk away from it.

I also began dressing nicely for his classes, hoping he would notice. I think he did, but even now, I can't be sure if it was in my head. It seemed like he lingered his eyes on me a little longer when I put in extra effort. It was embarrassing how much I wanted his attention, but I did. I started fantasizing about him sexually, even though he was so much older than me and, when I thought about it rationally, I definitely didn't want that. No matter how much I tried to push those thoughts away, they kept coming back, and I started to rely on those fantasies to become aroused.

I even began rehearsing imaginary conversations with him, imagining what I'd say if he ever confessed hidden feelings for me. It was exhausting, constantly swinging between wanting him and feeling shame about it, wondering how he felt, unsure of what was real and what wasn't.

Over time, it started to affect every part of my life. I fell behind in my coursework because I couldn't focus. My friends noticed I wasn't myself, but I didn't know how to explain it to them. How could I tell them I was obsessed with my lecturer? They would have laughed, and it would have been so embarrassing. He wasn't even objectively attractive. I felt isolated, like I was carrying this enormous secret I couldn't share. I started questioning myself constantly. Was this normal? Was I losing my mind? Why couldn't I just stop thinking about him?

Even after I finished his class, the feelings didn't just vanish. Not seeing him every week helped dull the intensity, but it didn't make them go away. I still think about him more often than I'd like. Sometimes I wonder what he's doing or imagine what might have happened if I'd said something, even though I know it's all fantasy.

To cope, I've had to find ways to manage my thoughts. Mindfulness helps a bit. It works to some degree, but it doesn't erase the feelings entirely. I still fantasize about him sexually and feel weird afterward. I hate that this still lingers, like a shadow I can't shake. I just want to feel normal again. I didn't choose to feel this way, and I wish I could let it go completely. I feel ashamed and stupid and just want to move on with my life.

To manage the grip of unexpressed feelings, it is crucial for the individual to discern whether expressing their emotions is appropriate or beneficial. In some cases, it may not be suitable to confess feelings, such as when doing so could harm existing relationships, disrupt professional boundaries, or create undue discomfort. In these situations, the individual must focus on managing their emotions privately through self-reflection, emotional regulation, and external support. In contexts where expressing these feelings is respectful, safe, and constructive, doing so can offer clarity and resolution. The key lies in thoughtful discernment of the circumstances.

When it is appropriate, confessing one's feelings can be a liberating and growth-oriented step. While the prospect of expressing emotions and obsession may be intimidating, and carries risks such as rejection or embarrassment, it provides the individual with an opportunity to transition their feelings from the realm of fantasy into reality. An honest conversation allows for a definitive response, either reciprocation or rejection, offering clarity that can pave the way for closure or a new beginning.

Taking this step is not without its challenges. Fear and anxiety about the outcome are natural, as the individual grapples with the vulnerability of sharing deeply personal emotions and obsessive thoughts. However, by choosing to share their experience, they create the possibility for authentic understanding. The desired person gains insight into their perspective, opening an opportunity for a genuine and respectful interaction. This act of openness can also be a powerful catalyst for personal growth, encouraging emotional resilience and self-awareness.

Confession serves two important purposes. First, it allows the individual to gain clarity and closure. If their feelings are mutual, it can open the door to a real relationship and resolve the limerence. If their feelings are not reciprocated, it helps them face reality and start healing. While it may be painful at first, confessing ends the uncertainty and ambiguity that sustain limerence. Secondly, sharing one's feelings encourages honest communication and mutual understanding. This open dialogue can cultivate empathy and respect, regardless of the outcome. It allows the desired person to gain insight into the limerent individual's emotions, fostering greater understanding and compassion. Even if the feelings are not reciprocated, the conversation can lay the groundwork for a more genuine and respectful relationship moving forward.

Unrequited Limerence

In the case of unreciprocated or unrequited limerence, the individual may find the courage to express their experience to the person they desire, only to be met with rejection. Whether this rejection is delivered with compassion or bluntness, it can be a deeply painful experience. The individual is forced to confront the reality that the connection they long for most is not available to them, and the emotional impact of this realization can be devastating.

Rejection can trigger a cascade of negative emotions, leaving the individual in a state of heartbreak, disappointment, and deep despair. The fantasies and hopes they had built around the person they desire are shattered, leaving them mourning not only the rejection but the loss of the imagined connection they had cherished. This sense of loss can feel overwhelming as they grapple with the now undeniable gap between their desires and reality.

The pain of rejection can also cause the individual to question their self-worth. It may evoke memories of past rejections or unresolved emotional wounds, amplifying the intensity of their grief. Navigating this experience requires self-reflection as the individual works through their shattered hopes and begins the process of healing.

Despite its painful nature, rejection in unrequited limerence carries a silver lining. The clear and definitive communication of lack of reciprocation extinguishes the hope that fuels limerence. By confronting the reality that their feelings are not mutual, the individual is given the opportunity to break free from the cycle of obsession and longing. While the loss of hope may initially be devastating, it is also the first step toward liberation from limerence.

Without the lingering glimmer of hope, the fantasies and obsessive thoughts that once consumed their mind begin to lose their grip. The individual starts to accept the truth of the situation, and over time, the intense emotional attachment begins to dissolve. The absence of reciprocation becomes a catalyst for letting go and moving forward.

Healing from unrequited limerence takes time and patience, but the clarity brought by rejection empowers the individual to redirect their focus. They can begin to invest their emotional energy into other areas of life, fostering personal growth and seeking connections that are more aligned with reality. The pain of rejection, though profound, becomes a stepping stone toward a healthier and more fulfilling future.

Case Study: Theresa

It was just after the pandemic, and I was finally returning to the office after months of working from home. The atmosphere at work felt different, with many people excited to reconnect in person. Among them was Lia, a new hire in my department. From the moment we started working together, I felt a strong connection.

For me, it was like the start of a fresh chapter. I had recently gone through a painful breakup and was eager to focus on building a new life. Lia and I bonded quickly. We often stayed late in the office, talking about everything from books and fitness to life experiences. She had this natural charisma, and the time we spent together was easy. We even started having lunch together most days, and I began to feel like she truly understood me.

Before long, our relationship changed into something closer and more intimate. At times, we would stay after work, walking together to the train station or just talking after everyone else had left. She would laugh at my jokes, touch my arm when we talked, and occasionally send me text messages outside of work. It was confusing because she was flirting with me but she never directly expressed feelings for me and I didn't know if she was into women in that way.

When Lia transferred to a different team, things changed. She became distant, replying to my messages less frequently and avoiding long conversations. It hurt more than I expected, but I couldn't seem to let it go. For months, I thought about her. I remembered the moments we had shared, trying to make sense of her sudden shift.

My work began to suffer. I struggled to stay focused in meetings and constantly found myself distracted by thoughts of her. I wasn't eating properly, working out, or looking after myself. I imagined scenarios where we would reconnect, where she would tell me that she felt the same way all along. Sometimes, I pictured us resuming our close friendship, just as it had been before. It was painful and frustrating to have these hopes and not know what was happening.

Eventually, I decided I had to address it. After weeks of overthinking, I sent her a message asking if we could meet. She agreed. I nervously told her how I'd been feeling, hoping for some clarity. She listened carefully and then told me the truth. She said she had never seen me as more than a friend and that my intensity with her had made her uncomfortable. She also mentioned that she had started seeing someone (a man), which was also why she had pulled away from the friendship.

Her words were devastating. I felt heartbroken and humiliated. But at the same time, there was a strange sense of relief in finally knowing where I stood. For so long, I'd clung to the hope that she might feel the same, but hearing the truth forced me to confront reality. I realized that I'd been holding onto a fantasy, sacrificing my wellbeing in the process. It was an emotional blow and a hard time for me, but at least I stopped obsessing. I'm glad I confronted her about it, otherwise I don't know if I might still be in that state. The rejection hurt, but at least I got clarity. I still find myself looking for her at work, but the fixation has become much less intense.

Ambiguous Reciprocity

One of the most challenging situations for a limerent individual is when the desired person's response to their confession is marked by ambiguity. If the reaction is mixed, uncertain, or suggests the possibility of future reciprocation, it can prolong the limerent experience. Even the smallest glimmer of hope can sustain fantasies, longing, and obsession.

Ambiguity keeps the flame of limerence alive, making closure impossible and perpetuating emotional distress. The lingering hope of a future where their feelings are returned hinders their ability to move on and let go.

As time passes, prolonged ambiguity has a detrimental impact on the limerent individual's mental health and emotional stability. The constant rollercoaster of emotions, alternating between fleeting hope and crushing disappointment, takes a toll, leaving them emotionally exhausted.

There are various potential reasons for this ambiguity. The desired person may genuinely be uncertain about their own emotions, struggling to understand or articulate their feelings. Alternatively, external factors such as poor timing or complicated life circumstances may contribute to their unclear response.

In more troubling cases, the ambiguity may stem from less innocent motivations. The desired person may have narcissistic traits and enjoy the attention and validation that comes from being the focus of someone's obsession. They may knowingly or unknowingly perpetuate the attachment for the ego boost it provides, regardless of the harm it causes to the limerent individual's wellbeing or relationships. This dynamic keeps the limerent individual trapped in a painful cycle of longing and uncertainty.

Case Study: Serena

I met Jason when we started working on the same project at work. We were friendly enough at first. Over time, our conversations shifted from work-related matters to more personal topics. Jason mentioned early on that he was married, and though I found him attractive I knew it could only ever be a work friendship. But as we continued to have enjoyable conversations, my feelings for him grew stronger.

We continued to spend time together at work, and over a few months we seemed to get closer. He made me feel seen. He complimented my ideas and asked for my input on projects, even when he didn't need to. He'd go out of his way to talk to me. Sometimes I'd catch him looking at me, he was touching me more casually and brushing against me as he moved by me. I started to wonder if he felt the same attraction I did. I knew it was wrong to want more from a married man, but I was very attracted to him.

One evening, we were both staying late to finish up a presentation. Alone in a meeting room, we were laughing about something trivial and then, completely unexpectedly, he leaned in and kissed me. I froze for a moment but then kissed him back. It was brief but passionate. It only lasted a few seconds and then he suddenly pulled back, mumbled something, and left the room, leaving me a bit in shock.

After that, I couldn't stop thinking about him. I replayed the kiss in my mind over and over and questioned everything. Was it just a fleeting impulse, or did it mean something more? Did he regret it, or was he as drawn to me as I was to him? His behavior at work gave me no answers. He was polite but very distant, avoiding one-on-one conversations and pretending nothing had happened.

I became completely fixated. I thought about him all the time and refused dates from available men so I could stay home, look at his social media, and fantasize about him. I started imagining what could be—him confessing his feelings and deciding to be with me—replaying the kiss over and over, and wondering how he felt.

I checked my phone constantly, desperate for a message from him, but it never came. The uncertainty was overwhelming. I felt like I was losing control and couldn't understand what was happening. I wasn't usually like this. I became very depressed and anxious.

The distance he put between us at work was painful, as we had been friends. He completely stayed away from me and acted like we didn't even know each other. This went on for about four months. Then, one evening as I was leaving the office, he texted me out of the blue. He asked if I wanted to have a drink with him, and I said yes. We went to a restaurant, and initially, it was just awkward small talk. Then I finally divulged everything. I told him I'd felt so confused since the kiss, that I felt such a pull toward him, and that I couldn't stop thinking about him and wondering endlessly how he felt about me.

He listened to what I was saying and didn't seem surprised. He admitted he also felt a spark between us and was very attracted to me. But then he said he was married and could never act on those feelings. He said it was complicated and that he couldn't do it because it wouldn't be right. But immediately after saying that, he reached over and touched me. He kind of ran his hand down the side of my arm. I didn't move. I was very confused and couldn't understand the mixed messages.

Then we left, and he offered me a lift home. We didn't talk much in the car. When we arrived at my apartment, he just parked the car and, without saying anything, followed me up to my apartment. He'd never come to my house before and didn't even ask if he could, but I let him. We went inside, and he completely changed. I'd never seen him like that before. So forward. He kissed me passionately, and we slept together. It was everything I had imagined it would be: passionate, intense, and emotional. For a moment afterward, I felt like all the fantasies I had built in my mind had come true and that he was also in love with me. But that changed very quickly. Pretty much as soon as we had finished, he went cold. He dressed very quickly, barely said goodbye, and walked out the door. I didn't hear from him all weekend, and I was completely beside myself. I tried calling him, but he didn't answer.

When I saw him at work the following week, he was back to being cold and distant. He avoided me entirely unless it was absolutely neces-sary, spoke to me very minimally as though we didn't know each other, and acted as if nothing had happened. I was devastated and felt very confused. I told my manager I wasn't feeling well and left work early. I couldn't handle being there with him like that after what had happened.

I went home and laid on my bed for several hours. I alternated between weeping and zoning out, just thinking about everything that had happened. I replayed every interaction in my mind, searching for answers. Did he regret what we had done? Was he trying to protect his marriage? Or had I misread everything from the beginning? Did I do something wrong? Did he not like my body? The uncertainty was unbearable. I still felt like I was in love with him, and I couldn't move on, even though I knew he was treating me badly. This was my only pastime at home for months, all while having to then see him at work, where he barely acknowledged my existence.

Then, suddenly, after months had passed, he texted me and asked to meet. I agreed, and when we met, he apologized, saying he had felt anx-ious and guilty about betraying his wife. He told me he actually did have feelings for me, and he was sorry. It was everything I wanted to hear.

The next day, it was back to him ignoring me like he barely knew me. It was so strange. After that, I decided he wasn't good for me and that I needed to stay away. It was very hard to stop thinking about him. Even though part of me hated him for how he was treating me, all I wanted was to be with him. I thought about him constantly and felt a physical aching to be with him again.

I felt isolated, ashamed, and heartbroken. The friends I spoke to about it didn't understand at all and couldn't believe I felt anything for this person who was treating me (and his wife) so badly. I stopped talking to friends about it because I was ashamed, but I kept thinking about him constantly and fantasizing about reconnecting. That's when I started to see a therapist to work on what was happening in my mind and the pain it was bringing up for me from childhood.

The next time he texted me and asked to meet, I said no. Even though I still want him to love me and I fantasize about us being together, I understand it's all in my mind and not something healthy for me. I still think about him a lot, and it's very conflicting. I know he is terrible, but at the same time I still want him. I compare all the men I try to date to him, and they always come up short. I don't talk to him at all anymore, but I still see him at work. I feel so bad for his wife and guilty about what I've done but he still has such a hold on me. The only reason I don't go back to him again is because I know what it would do to my mental health, and I can't bear it.

Limerence can manifest through a range of relational dynamics. Each experience is shaped by unique circumstances but shares common threads: emotional intensity, obsessive longing, and a powerful desire for reciprocation. How the limerent experience unfolds is determined not only by whether it is mutual, unexpressed, or unrequited, but also by the emotional intelligence, empathy, and responsiveness of the person who is desired. This highlights the importance of raising awareness about limerence as a psychologically distressing state. When recognized and understood, those on the receiving end of such feelings may be better equipped to respond with sensitivity, reducing the potential for long-term emotional harm.

9 I'm Not Supposed to Love You
Cultural and Ethical Condemnation

The way limerence is received and responded to by others has a profound impact on the experience itself. While some people may respond with compassion or understanding, others respond with condemnation. This is particularly true when feelings arise in contexts that society deems inappropriate, such as when an individual finds themselves captivated by someone for whom developing feelings is culturally or morally fraught.

When limerence toward someone considered off-limits takes hold, the emotional fallout can be more painful than if the feelings were for someone more socially acceptable. First, the individual must navigate the inner turmoil and complexity that limerence brings. Second, they are forced to confront the social and ethical implications of harboring and acting on such feelings. These consequences can include judgment, gossip, and shame, leading to social exclusion, reputational damage, and a loss of social standing. In the end, the limerent individual may be left feeling humiliated and isolated, managing their distress alone and in silence.

Norms

Societal expectations and norms shape who is considered an appropriate object of desire, influenced by factors such as availability, cultural background, religion, gender, power dynamics, and age. These frameworks not only influence who individuals feel permitted to pursue; they also create the conditions in which limerence can take hold and flourish. When certain connections are discouraged or forbidden, the tension between desire and restraint can intensify the experience. External barriers can amplify uncertainty, deepen longing, and heighten the emotional conflict experienced by the limerent individual.

Cultural expectations around relationships vary widely across the world. In many Western societies, the idea of *soulmates* romanticizes unattainable love and encourages the idealization of intense emotional experiences such as limerence. The belief in "the one" or "true love" is deeply embedded in cultural narratives, elevating forbidden or unreachable love to something aspirational. Within this framework, limerence can be perceived not as a source of distress, but as a sign of profound and meaningful connection, reinforcing its emotional intensity and appeal.

DOI: 10.4324/9781003563747-10

As soon as these feelings are directed toward someone deemed ethically or culturally inappropriate, however, the cultural attitude shifts. The same emotional intensity that was once idealized becomes condemned, leading to judgment and stigma. This shift is unjust, as individuals do not choose who they develop limerence for. The distressing obsession of limerence is frequently misunderstood and shamed, with the individual branded as morally flawed. The unfairness lies in being judged for thoughts and feelings they did not choose, which only deepens their emotional suffering and isolation.

The societal tendency to condemn limerent individuals for their feelings is akin to expressing to someone with obsessive–compulsive disorder (OCD) that their experience of obsession is only acceptable if it aligns with social norms. It is as if someone whose compulsion involves checking locks were to receive understanding and compassion, while another whose obsession centers on handwashing was met with judgment and exclusion. Similarly, a person with anxiety may be supported if their fears relate to public speaking, but not if they fear going outside. This is clearly irrational. Individuals do not choose the focus of their obsessions or anxieties and condemning them for it is deeply unfair.

During limerence, behaviors aimed at soothing the obsessive thoughts are often compulsive. Just as someone with OCD may feel driven to act on their obsessions despite knowing they are irrational, a limerent individual may struggle to suppress intrusive thoughts or resist certain actions, even when they fully recognize the social or ethical implications. This does not mean all behavior is beyond control or free from responsibility, but it does complicate the moral picture. Harsh judgment often overlooks this compulsive element, collapsing the distinction between willful misconduct and the actions of someone grappling with overwhelming psychological pressure.

It is therefore ironic that people who pride themselves on being empathetic and inclusive may still discriminate against limerent individuals based on the particular focus of their obsession. This kind of moral posturing overlooks the involuntary nature of limerence and reinforces stigma and shame. The absence of empathy compounds the suffering of those experiencing limerence, who are already grappling with intrusive thoughts and overwhelming emotions, and must now also face judgment, exclusion, and social sanctions.

Committed Relationships

One example of limerence that can lead to shame and social ostracization is when an individual in a committed relationship develops intense feelings for someone else. This situation brings significant distress, not only to the limerent individual, but also to their partner and others who may become aware of the emotional entanglement. The combination of guilt, emotional intensity, and societal judgment creates a profound internal struggle. Even when the feelings are not acted upon, the individual may feel as though they have already betrayed their partner, leading to confusion, secrecy, and shame.

This shame can arise from both actual external judgment and deeply internalized moral expectations. In some cases, the individual may face condemnation or rejection from others if their feelings are revealed. In other cases, they may experience intense self-judgment, shaped by a personal or cultural framework that deems such feelings inappropriate or wrong. Often, these two sources of distress are intertwined: internal conflict is magnified by the fear or reality of social consequences, and societal condemnation is reinforced by the individual's own sense of moral failure. Together, they create a psychological burden that persists even in the absence of outward behavior.

Another example is when limerence is centered around someone already in a committed relationship. If these feelings are discovered, the response from the desired person may be unpredictable, and their partner may experience distress, betrayal, or anger. In such cases, the limerent individual is frequently subject to judgment, both from others who may view their feelings as inappropriate and from themselves as they struggle with guilt or moral conflict. Strong feelings for someone else's partner are widely regarded as socially unacceptable, which can intensify the shame associated with them. Additionally, the existence of a prior relationship adds considerable complexity, making open communication difficult and reducing the likelihood of resolution. These barriers can heighten the limerent individual's longing and internal conflict.

The moral boundaries of monogamy form a central part of many cultural and religious frameworks. In Judeo-Christian traditions, for instance, they are set out explicitly in the Ten Commandments: "Thou shalt not covet thy neighbor's wife" (Exodus 20:17, as cited in Kaplan, 1981). Such expectations around fidelity and loyalty reinforce the idea that even private feelings may be morally wrong. When limerence arises in these contexts, the internal conflict between desire and conscience becomes particularly painful. The presence of external barriers, combined with internal guilt, can sustain and intensify the limerent state over extended periods, contributing to ongoing emotional turmoil and distress.

Cultural and Religious Barriers

Another example of limerence centered on someone considered inappropriate arises when cultural or religious differences create judgment or external barriers to the relationship. In many Hindu communities, for example, arranged marriages remain a valued tradition, with families taking an active role in selecting partners based on caste, social status, and horoscope compatibility. In Islamic culture, marrying within the faith is strongly encouraged, reflecting the emphasis placed on shared religious values and beliefs. Similarly, Jewish traditions uphold endogamy as a means of preserving cultural and religious heritage.

Similarly, same-sex attraction presents an additional, often deeply challenging, barrier within many religious traditions, particularly among followers of the conservative or fundamentalist branches of Christianity, Judaism, and

Islam. In these contexts, limerence directed toward a person of the same sex may lead to profound internal conflict, secrecy, or guilt due to religious teachings that frame such desires as sinful or unnatural. In some communities, the discovery of these feelings can result in outright rejection, family estrangement, abuse, or pressure to conform to heterosexual expectations, regardless of the emotional authenticity or intensity of the limerent experience.

Cultural barriers can also operate independently of religion. For example, in some East Asian communities, family expectations may strongly emphasize marrying within one's ethnic or national group. A Chinese family, for instance, might prefer that their child marry someone not only Chinese but also from a specific region or background, such as mainland China, Taiwan, or a particular dialect group. These expectations can be shaped by cultural values around lineage, compatibility, and tradition. In immigrant contexts, such expectations may shift, soften, or, in some cases, become even more rigid as families attempt to preserve cultural identity in a new environment. For example, a second-generation Australian person may face different pressures from their Australian-based family than from relatives still living in Malaysia or China. Limerence that crosses these cultural boundaries can provoke complex emotional and interpersonal struggles, especially when it evokes fears of assimilation, loss of heritage, or cultural betrayal.

When individuals from these backgrounds experience strong feelings for someone outside their religious or cultural group, they may face significant internal and external conflict. The limerent individual is caught between the intensity of their longing and the expectations that dictate whom they are permitted to love. In some cases, the very presence of disapproval from family or community can increase the emotional intensity of the relationship, as external barriers have been shown to heighten feelings of romantic love (Driscoll et al., 1972). Navigating these boundaries while managing the emotional grip of limerence becomes an immensely difficult task. The clash between personal desire and communal norms creates deep distress, as the individual struggles to reconcile their emotions with the religious or cultural pressures imposed upon them.

Power Dynamics

Power dynamics can significantly shape the experience of limerence, particularly when the person experiencing these feelings holds a position of authority or influence, such as a teacher, boss, therapist, or mentor. Limerence in such contexts creates a complex and emotionally charged situation. These relationships tend to attract scrutiny and social condemnation, as the inherent imbalance raises legitimate concerns about consent, professional ethics, and the potential misuse of power. The limerent individual may struggle with shame, guilt, and internal conflict, especially when their role requires emotional neutrality or professional distance.

In these cases, the distressing nature of limerence is amplified by the ethical tension of desiring someone over whom they hold authority. The individual may fear acting inappropriately, breaching trust, or compromising their integrity or position, yet still feel unable to control their emotional fixation.

The reverse dynamic, where the limerent individual is in a subordinate position such as a student, employee, or patient, presents a different but equally complex set of challenges. In these situations, the limerent individual may idealize the authority figure, projecting onto them qualities such as wisdom, strength, or emotional safety. This can intensify emotional dependency and fantasy, creating a perceived intimacy that does not reflect the reality of the relationship. The subordinate position also increases vulnerability, particularly if the authority figure is unaware of the attachment or fails to maintain appropriate boundaries.

In both configurations, the imbalance of power complicates the experience of limerence and increases the potential for emotional harm. The distress is both internal and shaped by cultural narratives, institutional expectations, and the risk of perceived or actual boundary violations. The emotional charge created by secrecy, risk, or ethical tension can intensify limerent feelings, heightening arousal and desire in ways that do not necessarily reflect the reality of the relationship. Research has shown that emotional arousal, including fear, can increase sexual or romantic attraction by amplifying physiological responses (Dutton & Aron, 1974). In limerent experiences involving power imbalances, these effects may be especially pronounced, making it more difficult to distinguish between a genuine emotional connection and a reaction to the charged context.

Age Differences

Age difference is another factor that can complicate limerent relationships. When there is a significant gap between individuals, societal norms and personal values may come into conflict. For example, when a younger woman develops limerence for a much older man, the social pressure to avoid the relationship can become overwhelming and add to distress. Similarly, an older woman who develops intense feelings for a much younger man may face judgment, particularly in cultures where significant age gaps are frowned upon regardless of gender. In both cases, concerns about power imbalance, social perception, and the potential consequences for both parties create a complex moral and ethical dilemma. Limerence in such contexts can be intensified by emotional stakes, amplifying confusion, longing, and inner conflict, and making it even more difficult to navigate the situation with clarity or peace of mind.

Double Standard

There is a clear double standard in how society responds to different psychological and emotional experiences. In recent years, there has been growing awareness and compassion toward mental health conditions such as depression, anxiety, and trauma-related disorders. Neurodiversity is increasingly recognized and discussed, reflecting a broader cultural willingness to accept that internal experiences are not always within a person's control, and that shame and stigma only make suffering worse.

But when it comes to limerence, particularly when feelings are directed toward someone unavailable or socially inappropriate, the cultural response is often far less compassionate. Instead of empathy, limerent individuals are more likely to be met with judgment, moral condemnation, and exclusion. Their experiences are dismissed as obsessive, selfish, or manipulative, rather than understood as part of a distressing psychological state shaped by emotional vulnerability and unmet attachment needs.

This disparity reflects a deeper discomfort with emotional states that challenge social norms. While there is growing acceptance of internal struggles such as anxiety, grief, or addiction, there is still little space for compassion when someone's longing falls outside what is considered acceptable. The limerent person becomes a target of gossip, moral scrutiny, or character judgment, regardless of whether they have acted on their feelings.

None of this implies that harmful behavior should be excused. Just as individuals with depression or addiction are held responsible for how they manage their condition and treat others, limerent individuals must also be accountable for their actions. But accountability is not the same as moral condemnation. Recognizing that limerence involves intrusive thoughts, compulsive behavior, and impaired judgment allows for a more balanced response, one that respects ethical boundaries while still acknowledging psychological distress.

Gender Differences

The double standard surrounding limerence is not only selective but also deeply gendered. Societal norms frequently hold women to stricter standards than men when it comes to emotional expression and desire. Women are expected to embody composure, modesty, and self-restraint. When their emotions fall outside these expectations, especially in the form of obsessive or socially inappropriate desire, they are labeled as irrational, weak, or morally flawed. These cultural biases trivialize women's emotional struggles, dismissing them as excessive or unstable, which only deepens their sense of shame and isolation.

This condemnation intensifies when a woman's limerent feelings are directed toward someone considered off-limits, such as a married man or someone outside her social or cultural sphere. Society tends to view such emotions as a personal failing, as though she is to blame for feelings she did not choose. In contrast, men who experience similar feelings are more likely to be excused or even admired. When male limerence is directed toward someone unavailable, it is reframed as romantic persistence, passion, or noble determination, aligning with cultural ideals that celebrate masculine pursuit and desire.

These unequal perceptions have historical roots in patriarchal systems that sought to control female sexuality and emotional agency. Before the rise of patriarchal monogamy, many goddess-worshipping societies celebrated wom-en's fertility and sexuality, with lineage passed through the maternal line. As patriarchal norms took hold, women's bodies and emotions were increasingly regulated in order to secure male lineage and inheritance (Lerner, 1986). This legacy is still visible in cultural practices such as women and children tak-ing the father's surname. While these customs are changing in some places, they remain widely practiced and continue to symbolize male authority and ownership.

Patriarchal religious traditions further entrenched these standards. In the Hebrew Bible, for example, a woman accused of adultery was to be brought before a priest, have her hair uncovered, and be made to drink bitter water. If found guilty, her belly would swell and she would be marked as cursed (Num-bers 5:11–31; Kaplan, 1981). These rituals applied only to women, reinforc-ing a societal fixation on female fidelity while overlooking male accountability. Cultural narratives further shaped this imbalance by promoting the image of the "temptress," blaming women for male transgressions and framing their desires as inherently dangerous.

This gendered double standard remains deeply embedded in contempo-rary culture. Norms shaped by traditional gender roles still portray women's emotional intensity, particularly in unrequited or taboo contexts, as unstable or melodramatic. Men's similar behavior, however, is more likely to be inter-preted as passionate or assertive. Media representations reinforce these ideas, frequently casting male characters' obsessive feelings as romantic and heroic, while portraying women in similar roles as desperate, unstable, or comical.

These patterns are grounded in a binary understanding of gender, and those who do not identify within that binary may find their experiences of limerence even more marginalized or misread. The dominant cultural scripts for how desire is supposed to look often fail to account for gender diversity, leaving some people entirely outside the frame of recognition or understanding.

Impact of Stigma

The isolation experienced by limerent individuals in these situations has deeply detrimental effects. Cut off from their support networks of friends, family, and community, they are left to grapple with overwhelming obsession in confu-sion and solitude. This disconnection amplifies their suffering, compounding emotional pain with loneliness and despair.

In some cases, limerent individuals may intentionally withdraw or emotion-ally distance themselves from others, attempting to hide their obsession out of a deep sense of shame. The shaming and condemnation they face from their community during a time when they are already grappling with severe mental health challenges can permanently damage these relationships.

For limerent individuals, particularly those with insecure attachment styles, this rejection reinforces existing fears about relationships and trust. They may already struggle to feel safe in their connections, and this judgment can serve

as proof that others are unreliable or unsafe. This further deepens their aliena-
tion and may strengthen the core belief that their fears around relationships
are justified, compounding the emotional struggles caused by limerence.

The condemnation of limerent individuals in such cases may mirror broader
societal discomfort with emotions and desires that deviate from established
norms. While these norms serve to preserve social order and uphold traditional values, they can simultaneously inflict considerable harm on those who
find themselves positioned outside these boundaries. Limerent individuals do
not choose their psychological state, yet, they are burdened with moral judgment and forced to navigate their obsession and distress in addition to the
responses of shame, stigma, and exclusion from the community.

Recognizing limerence as a condition shaped by attachment trauma and
neurobiological processes offers the potential for a more compassionate cultural response. Rather than treating limerence as a character flaw, society
might begin to understand it as a deeply distressing psychological state that is
not resolved through condemnation but with care, insight, and support, while
still holding individuals responsible for how they manage their actions and
boundaries, as is expected in the context of other mental health conditions.

References

Driscoll, R., Davis, K. E., & Lipetz, M. E. (1972). Parental interference and romantic
love: The Romeo and Juliet effect. *Journal of Personality and Social Psychology, 24*(1),
1–10. https://doi.org/10.1037/h0033373

Dutton, D. G., & Aron, A. P. (1974). Some evidence for heightened sexual attraction
under conditions of high anxiety. *Journal of Personality and Social Psychology, 30*(4),
510–517. https://doi.org/10.1037/h0037031

Kaplan, A. (1981). *The Living Torah: A new translation based on traditional Jewish
sources (The Five Books of Moses).* Moznaim Pub Corp.

Lerner, G. (1986). *The creation of patriarchy.* Oxford University Press.

10 Take This Longing from My Tongue

Limerence in Art, Literature, Music, and Film

Artistic expression across time and civilizations has mirrored and molded cultural perceptions of love, encompassing its divine elements as well as its more obsessive, consuming forms. Across mediums such as visual art, literature, music, and film, love emerges as a force of both inspiration and torment, with many portrayals glorifying and legitimizing its more pathological dimensions. These depictions have played a central role in constructing collective understandings of love and desire, transforming infatuation, longing, and emotional dependency into objects of beauty and fascination. For many artists, love serves as both muse and affliction. Creative expression offers a way to process emotional intensity and reshape personal suffering into coherent, meaningful narrative (Pennebaker, 1997). Many works arise from the impulse to ease longing. These expressions have shaped how societies perceive love and yearning, contributing to the cultural legacy of limerence and offering insight into its emotional depth and complexity.

Visual Art

During the Renaissance, love and beauty played a central role in the visual arts, inspiring works that explored both the earthly and transcendent dimensions of human emotion. A quintessential example is Sandro Botticelli's *The Birth of Venus* (Figure 10.1), painted around the mid-1480s. In this masterpiece, the goddess Venus emerges from the sea on a giant shell, symbolizing the arrival of love and beauty into the world. The sea, associated with the subconscious and the depths of human feeling, serves as a powerful backdrop, framing Venus's emergence as an embodiment of idealized love. Botticelli's portrayal presents love and beauty as physical and spiritual forces, positioning them as muses that guide artistic inspiration.

Another compelling example is Henri-Léopold Lévy's *Young Woman and Death*, painted in 1876 (Figure 10.2). Figure 10.2 depicts a woman being carried away by a winged figure, traditionally interpreted as Death, while a man kneels beside her, desperately trying to hold her back. This powerful composition symbolizes the tension between life and death, with Death drawing the woman into an otherworldly realm and severing her ties to the physical world

DOI: 10.4324/9781003563747-11

Figure 10.1 The Birth of Venus (La nascita di Venere), c. 1485. Sandro Botticelli. Tempera on canvas, 172.5 cm × 279 cm. Uffizi Galleries (Galleria dei Uffizi), Florence. Digital reproduction: Google Arts and Culture. Public domain.

and the man who clings to her. The scene can also be read as an allegory for the seductive pull of fantasy. The woman's surrender reflects how immersion in idealized longing can remove individuals from reality and emotional presence.

John Everett Millais' 1852 painting *Ophelia* (Figure 10.3) presents a haunting depiction of Shakespeare's tragic heroine from *Hamlet*, capturing the moment she succumbs to the river's depths. Floating amid lush, intricately detailed foliage, Ophelia clutches flowers with symbolic meanings: poppies for death, daisies for innocence, and willows for forsaken love. Her open mouth and distant gaze evoke seductive passivity, suggesting she yields to the weight of emotion. Millais transforms her into an emblem of beauty entangled with tragedy.

The river becomes a metaphor for emotional submersion. As Ophelia drifts into the current, she is lost in a dream detached from reality. Her surrender reflects how limerent individuals can relinquish agency, consumed by fantasy and longing. Through its emotional depth, *Ophelia* captures the pull to disappear into idealized love, suspended between beauty and despair.

These works, and many others, serve as powerful visual representations of different aspects of limerence. They depict a passive surrender to fantasy, with figures drifting, drowning, or being carried away. This imagery evokes a submission to obsession and emotional overwhelm. The boundary between reality and imagination blurs. The individual is pulled into a dreamlike state, consumed by feeling and cut off from the tangible world. These images reflect the consuming force of limerence, where intense emotions distort perception and disconnect the individual from reality.

Figure 10.2 Young Woman and Death (*La jeune fille et la mort*), 1900. Henri-Léopold
Lévy. Oil on canvas, 346 cm × 312.5 cm. Museum of Fine Arts of Nancy
(Musée des Beaux-Arts de Nancy), France. Public domain.

Figure 10.3 Ophelia, c. 1851. John Everett Millais. Tate, presented by Sir Henry Tate, 1894. Photo: Tate.

Literature

Literature contains countless portrayals of idealized and obsessive infatuation. Poets, authors, and playwrights have explored the realm of limerence, capturing its intensity and torment. These works expose the euphoric highs and crushing lows of idealized love, giving voice to those caught in cycles of longing, fantasy, and emotional fixation.

Dante Alighieri's *The Divine Comedy* offers one of the earliest and most influential examples. Written between 1308 and 1320, the epic poem takes the reader on a transformative journey as Dante, guided by the Roman poet Virgil, embarks on a quest from the "dark wood" toward redemption, inspired by his beloved Beatrice. Throughout the poem's first part, *Inferno*, Dante travels through the descending circles of hell, encountering vivid punishments and torments that reflect human sin. His journey reaches the darkest point at the bottom of hell, where he confronts Lucifer.

In the second part, *Purgatorio*, he continues upward as he and Virgil emerge at the base of the Mountain of Purgatory, where souls undergo purification in preparation for their ascent to heaven. At the end of *Purgatorio* Virgil departs, and Dante is reunited with Beatrice, who becomes his guide through the third part of the poem, *Paradiso*. She leads him through the successive, ascending spheres of Paradise, where Dante encounters saints, angels, and divine wisdom. Finally, in the Empyrean, the highest level of heaven, Dante is granted a momentary, transcendent vision of the glory of God. This revelation becomes the ultimate culmination of his journey, leaving him transformed.

The Divine Comedy has deep connections to the experience of limerence, as Dante's journey is guided by his idealized love for Beatrice. Throughout the text, Beatrice remains distant, idealized, and untouchable, an archetype of unconsummated devotion. Dante's descent into hell and ascent into heaven serve as symbols for the agonizing lows and euphoric highs experienced in limerence. While his journey is fraught with suffering and reflections of sin, it ultimately leads to spiritual growth and enlightenment, reflecting how limerence, despite its anguish, can serve as a transformative force within the psyche.

In other parts of the world, we find similar examples of themes of potent longing and desire. Sufi poetry, in particular, is saturated with expressions of deep love and yearning, blending the physical with the divine. One such poet is Rumi (Jalal ad-Din Muhammad Rumi), a 13th-century Persian poet and mystic whose works are among the most celebrated in world literature. Rumi's writings vividly capture the ecstasy, yearning, and longing associated with intense love, using metaphors of human passion to convey spiritual union and divine connection. His poetry transcends time and culture, offering insights into the universal nature of desire and the transformative power of longing (Schimmel, 1975).

In his poem *I've Come Again*, Rumi writes:

how dare you to
let someone like me
intoxicated with love
enter your house

you must know better
if I enter
I'll break all this and
destroy all that
        (Rumi, ca. 1270/1994)

This passage encapsulates Rumi's intense, defiant longing, blending themes of spiritual intoxication, passionate love, and frustration with worldly limitations. The vivid imagery of destruction and rebellion reflects the overwhelming and sometimes destructive power of desire. Rumi's poetry portrays love as an all-consuming force that breaks societal and cosmic boundaries, resonating deeply with the emotional experience of limerence.

Reflecting the idealized and otherworldly nature of secret yearning, Rumi writes in his poem *Secret Places*:

Lovers find secret places
inside this violent world
where they make transactions
with beauty.

Reason says, Nonsense.
I have walked and measured the walls here.
There are no places like that.

Love says, There are.
Reason sets up a market
and begins doing business.

Love has more hidden work.
Hallaj steps away from the pulpit
and climbs the stairs of the gallows.

Lovers feel a truth inside themselves
that rational people keep denying.

It is reasonable to say, Surrender
is just an idea that keeps people from leading their lives.

Love responds, No. This thinking
is what is dangerous.

(Rumi, ca. 1270/1995)

This passage highlights the profound tension between reality and the secret, otherworldly realms created by idealized love. Rumi speaks to the way intense emotions can lead to the construction of a secret, imagined reality, one where beauty and connection exist beyond the constraints of logic. This resonates deeply with the nature of limerence, where individuals idealize the desired person and escape into a world of fantasy that seems more vivid and meaningful than reality.

Rumi's exploration of longing and desire can be traced to various sources, with one significant factor being his profound spiritual connection and insatiable yearning for the Divine. His writings, often interpreted as dialogues with God, vividly capture the essence of divine longing and mystical union. However, Rumi's poetic repertoire encompasses more than celestial aspirations alone. Amid his transcendent verses, there are moments that reflect distinctly human experiences of infatuation and yearning. These glimpses reveal themes of intense longing and the complexities of human relationships, which he himself may have grappled with and which resonate with the emotional landscape of limerence (Schimmel, 1975).

Another literary figure who made significant contributions to the exploration of longing and desire is Anaïs Nin, a French-born American writer active in the early 20th century. Her writings explore passion, desire, and the complexities of human relationships, offering a nuanced portrayal of obsessive love. Nin's works center on intimate and intense connections between characters, vividly capturing the enthralling and consuming nature of infatuation. Through her introspective and poetic prose, she intricately examines the dynamics of love, longing, and obsession (Nin, 1966).

In addition to her numerous literary works, Nin engaged in a remarkable and enduring correspondence with American writer Henry Miller. Spanning several decades, their exchange resulted in a collection of deeply personal and intimate letters that illuminate the intricacies of their complex relationship. Both Nin and Miller were married to other people throughout this time, which complicated their connection and added a layer of forbidden longing. Rather than remaining unfulfilled, their limerence was acted upon, manifesting in both emotional and sexual intimacy. Their relationship was shaped by the tension of secrecy and transgression as much as by genuine affection. Marked by intense passion, intellectual synergy, and profound emotional depth, their letters explore themes of yearning, desire, taboo, and the interplay between love and creative expression.

Through their candid and vulnerable correspondence, Nin and Miller shared their deepest thoughts, vulnerabilities, and desires, weaving a tapestry of emotional intimacy that continues to captivate readers. In a letter to Nin in 1932, Miller writes:

> When you return, I am going to give you one literary fuck fest—that means fucking and talking and talking and fucking—and a bottle of Anjou in between—or a Vermouth Cassis. Anaïs, I am going to open your very groins. God forgive me if this letter is ever opened by mistake. I can't help it. I want you. I love you. You're food and drink to me—the whole bloody machinery, as it were. Lying on top of you is one thing, but getting close to you is another. I feel close to you, one with you, you're mine whether it is acknowledged or not. Every day I wait now is torture. I am counting them slowly, painfully. I don't know when you return—the 7th or the 15th? But make it as soon as you can. Be unselfish—yes, I am asking you to. Make a sacrifice. I need you. This long Sunday—how will I ever get through it? It is just killing time.
>   (Miller, as cited in Nin, 1987, p. 125)

This letter illustrates the raw and unfiltered intensity of their connection, marked by passion, fixation, and an almost unbearable sense of anticipation. The vivid language and emotional urgency exemplify the depths of their mutual longing. Miller's words reveal physical and emotional yearning as well as the almost torturous experience of waiting, a hallmark of the limerent state.

In a letter to Miller during the same period, Nin writes:

> I want to love you wildly. I don't want words, but inarticulate cries, meaningless, from the bottom of my most primitive being, that flow from my belly like honey. A piercing joy that leaves me empty, conquered, silenced.
>   (Nin, 1987, p. 131)

This vivid and unrestrained expression of desire exemplifies the euphoric and fanatical intensity of the limerent experience. Decades later, after extended periods of geographical and emotional distance, Nin reflects on the enduring power of such an intoxicating connection, writing: "To think of him in the middle of the day lifts me out of ordinary living" (Nin, 1966, p. 237).

These examples offer just a glimpse into the vast body of literary works that explore the depths of longing, obsession, and emotional fixation, preserving these states through art and contributing richly to the cultural legacy of limerence.

Music

Music is another powerful medium for the exploration of limerence, with countless songs dedicated to its themes. From classical compositions to contemporary pop, artists have channeled obsessive longing, idealization, and emotional fixation into their work.

In the classical tradition, Beethoven's Piano Sonata No. 14 in C-sharp minor, commonly known as the *Moonlight Sonata* (Beethoven, 1801/2012), offers a striking example. Composed in 1801 and dedicated to his much younger student, Countess Juliw "Giulietta" Guicciardi, the piece has long been interpreted as a lament of unrequited love. The first movement's somber, meditative tone evokes a quiet sorrow and emotional restraint, building into waves of tension that mirror the intensifying turmoil of longing. The piece is widely considered an emotional confession of a love he could not realize, its melancholic beauty echoing the pain of desiring someone who is unattainable (Cooper, 2001).

A more recent artist whose work profoundly embodies the limerent experience is Leonard Cohen. He writes about love in a way that elevates it to a state of reverence, sacrifice, and emotional devotion so raw it borders on religious. Cohen's lyrics unite sensuality and sanctity. His longing is never casual. It kneels, prays, burns, and endures. In his song *Light as a Breeze* (Cohen, 1992), he conjures the image of worship as a metaphor for obsession, with the desired other elevated to the level of the divine. His surrender is ritualistic. In *Take This Longing* (Cohen, 1974), he speaks from the depths of desire, longing to see the other undone, not out of cruelty, but as a plea for intimacy and union. Through his songs, his longing is expressed as both hunger and surrender. His lyrics offer a rare and unfiltered glimpse into the torment of a mind consumed by obsessive unresolved longing.

Bob Dylan, by contrast, portrays longing with a kind of weathered despair. There is cynicism in his love, but also loyalty. His obsession has grown tired yet refuses to let go. In *Love Sick* (Dylan, 1997a), Dylan's admission that he is sick of "this kind of love" speaks not to apathy, but to the exhausting nature of unrelenting desire that continues to grip the psyche long after it has ceased to be wanted. In *Make You Feel My Love*, he offers total emotional sacrifice, declaring a willingness to endure pain, hunger, and humiliation for the desired other to feel and receive his longing. His love is scratched at the edges, worn thin from use, but still burning on the altar of his songs.

Neil Young's portrayal of longing moves with a softer, more spectral quality. His expression is dreamlike, filled with gentle projections rather than explicit need. In *Harvest* (Young, 1972), the fantasy remains untouched by reality. He sings of imagined connection and, like the Demon Lover archetype, he offers only the vague promise of a man rather than the man himself. His desire lives in the air; fragile, distant, and softly flickering. Where Dylan and Cohen dive into the ache, Young floats above it, caught in the wistfulness of love that exists only in the mind.

Jeff Buckley delivers longing as emotional possession. His voice trembles with vulnerability and surrender, offering no distance between himself and his need. In *Lover, You Should've Come Over* (Buckley, 1994), he collapses under the weight of desire, confessing hunger with a kind of sacred grief. His yearning is not metaphorical; it is embodied. His vocals stretch and quake with the ache of separation, every note a cry for reunion. Buckley's fixation feels like drowning, beautiful, immersive, and devastating.

Nina Simone brings a fierce, almost mystical intensity to her portrayals of longing and obsession. In *I Put a Spell on You* (Simone, 1965), she channels the desperation of unreciprocated desire into a hypnotic incantation, turning love into a force of possession. Her rendition of *Lilac Wine* (Simone, 1966) captures the intoxicating haze of yearning, where reality dissolves into a dreamscape. Simone's voice, steeped in emotional complexity, draws the listener in to the seductive and painful pull of her yearning.

Billie Holiday's music reflects the complexities of love, deception, and emotional endurance. In *Don't Explain* (Holiday, 1946), she addresses betrayal with quiet resignation, embodying the paradox of loving someone who wounds you. Her phrasing, always raw and nuanced, gives voice to the pain and persistence of obsessive love. She embodies the enduring nature of limerence even once the pathology has been laid bare.

Chris Isaak's *Wicked Game* (Isaak, 1989) is an anthem of limerent torment. Its melancholy guitar and Isaak's aching vocals capture the despair of falling for someone who brings pain. The lyrics lament the cruelty of being made to dream of someone who never arrives. The song immerses listeners in the bitter beauty of desire that cannot be realized, where dreams become a haunting affliction.

Contemporary pop continues this tradition with compelling force. Kylie Minogue's *Can't Get You Out of My Head* (Minogue, 2001) turns repetition into rhythm, echoing the looping thoughts that define limerent fixation. Taylor Swift's *Don't Blame Me* (Swift, 2017) speaks of love as a drug, confessing a willingness to lose sanity for the high of emotional reciprocation and union. Billie Eilish's *My Strange Addiction* (Eilish, 2019) nods to limerence as a pathological state her doctors don't understand. These songs, wrapped in polished production and catchy melodies, embed complex emotional realities within the fabric of mainstream culture.

Across genres and generations, music gives voice to the compulsion, fantasy, and longing that define limerence. These are just a few of the countless examples that explore love in its most obsessive and idealized forms. Through melody and verse, artists make limerence audible, turning private suffering into public art, and transforming torment into something beautiful. These songs hint at the underlying pathology of obsessive infatuation while also glorifying its intensity, capturing both the beauty and the distress of profound longing and emotional fixation.

Film

Film is another significant cultural and artistic medium that explores themes of idealized love and emotional fixation through storytelling and visual expression. From early childhood, many audiences are introduced to ideas about love through Disney's animated fairytales. Many of these stories are adapted from older European folktales, particularly those collected by the Brothers Grimm, yet the Disney versions significantly alter their tone and message (Zipes, 1994). Darker themes of violence, ambiguity, and moral complexity are replaced with simplified narratives that position romantic love as the ultimate resolution. In these adaptations, love is portrayed as pure, transformative, and destined. Female characters are often cast as passive, virtuous, and emotionally devoted, while male characters arrive as rescuers or rewards.

Across classic titles such as Cinderella (1950), Sleeping Beauty (1959), The Little Mermaid (1989), and Beauty and the Beast (1991), love is frequently presented as immediate and all-consuming. Protagonists are expected to wait, hope, or suffer quietly until they are chosen. Ariel gives up her voice and identity to pursue a prince she has never spoken to. Belle falls in love with her captor, with her patience and emotional labor framed as redemptive. These portrayals embed the idea that romantic longing is noble, that suffering in silence is meaningful, and that emotional dependency is rewarded. The intensity of desire is equated with the value of the connection, even when the relationship lacks communication or reciprocity.

However, recently Disney has undergone a notable transformation. Contemporary films such as Moana (2016), Brave (2012), Encanto (2021), and Frozen (2013) represent a marked shift in the portrayal of female protagonists. In these narratives, love interests are absent or secondary. Themes such as self-actualization, sibling love, and emotional resilience take center stage. Films like Brave and Moana explicitly reject romantic subplots, and in Frozen, the central act of true love is between sisters, not lovers. This evolution aligns with broader feminist discourses and societal shifts, as noted in recent scholarship (Schiele et al., 2020).

This transition not only reflects changing values but is also a response to criticism. Earlier portrayals have been accused of reinforcing patriarchal norms and passive femininity. In response, Disney's more recent characters actively shape their destinies, pursue leadership, and challenge gendered expectations (Schiele et al., 2020). Even as newer stories challenge outdated ideals, many people still carry emotional imprints from earlier portrayals that equate obsessive romantic longing with true love. This contributes to the ongoing cultural confusion between limerence and healthy emotional connection.

This cultural blurring between limerence and love is reinforced by romantic comedies and dramas, which often present obsessive or emotionally intense behavior as meaningful or admirable rather than as signs of psychological distress. Love Actually (Curtis, 2003) provides a salient example. One storyline features Mark, who is secretly in love with his best friend's wife, Juliet. He films her obsessively on her wedding day and later shows up at her house with cue cards confessing his love.

When the film was released, this scene was widely seen as romantic. In more recent years, however, many viewers have critiqued Mark's behavior as intrusive or inappropriate. While this reassessment is important, it is equally necessary to consider the psychological distress underlying his actions. Rather than simply condemning or romanticizing him, a more nuanced reading would acknowledge the internal struggle and emotional confusion that can accompany limerence, helping to clarify how such experiences are often dismissed and misunderstood.

This example illustrates how limerent behavior is often romanticized in media, creating a template where obsessive longing is seen as evidence of true love. This narrative can mislead viewers into equating emotional turmoil with romantic depth. The problem is not that fiction includes dramatic or fantastical elements, since audiences understand that stories are heightened for emotional effect. The issue arises when repeated exposure to these templates begins to normalize maladaptive behavior.

Many films across genres, including Casablanca (Curtiz, 1942), Gone with the Wind (Fleming, 1939), Eternal Sunshine of the Spotless Mind (Gondry, 2004), Silver Linings Playbook (Russell, 2012), 500 Days of Summer (Webb, 2009), and La La Land (Chazelle, 2016), portray intense infatuation as meaningful and transformative. Characters endure suffering, miscommunication, and emotional chaos, yet these qualities are often framed as signs of romantic authenticity. In some cases, limerent fixation becomes a stand-in for love itself.

Part of this appeal lies in narrative structure. Romantic tension drives plot, sustains audience interest, and creates emotional payoff. Readers and viewers often seek heightened emotion and drama rather than mundane stability. However, when such narratives are interpreted outside of their fictional context, they can distort expectations about real relationships. This distortion becomes problematic when limerent individuals look to these templates for validation, mistaking obsessive longing for healthy connection.

Ultimately, media portrayals shape collective ideas about love. When limerent patterns are repeatedly framed as romantic ideals, they can influence how people perceive their own emotional experiences. This confusion may downplay the distress and dysfunction of limerence, making it harder for individuals to recognize it as a psychological disturbance. It can also set unrealistic expectations for romantic connection, leading people to believe that intensity, suffering, and pathology are necessary components of love, rather than signs of a psychological condition in need of understanding and support.

Legacy of Limerence

The cultural legacy of limerence includes a long history of artistic expression that presents longing as sacred, transcendent, and deeply meaningful. Across literature, music, visual art, and film, devotion and emotional intensity are portrayed as markers of profound inner life and spiritual depth. These portrayals reflect limerent experiences and emerge from them. Many of these artists may have themselves been experiencing limerence and relied on their artistic expression as a way to soothe or survive their suffering. For individuals in a limerent state, such works can feel deeply resonant, as though the external world has given form to an internal dreamscape. The art appears to affirm the experience, offering a kind of emotional mirror in which the intensity of desire is validated, even sanctified. In this way, limerent individuals may find comfort and meaning in these cultural expressions, which seem to speak the language of their own longing.

Yet the cultural legacy of limerence can also obscure the more distressing reality of the experience. While artistic portrayals elevate obsessive desire into something beautiful and poetic, they also normalize patterns that, in practice, involve psychological distress, impaired functioning, and prolonged emotional suffering. Once these portrayals become embedded in cultural consciousness, limerence is less likely to be recognized as a complex and painful state. Instead, it is framed as a normal, even desirable, expression of romantic feeling. This cultural script not only dismisses the real suffering of those caught in obsessive longing, casting them as simply "in love," but also distorts ideas of what love should feel like. People who do not experience limerence may come to believe that real love must feel dramatic, overwhelming, or agonizing. This can create confusion, dissatisfaction, or even lead to the pursuit of emotionally unhealthy relationships in the hope of matching a standard they have been taught to admire. As a result, the boundary between psychological disturbance and romantic devotion becomes increasingly blurred, making it more difficult to recognize limerence as a distinct and disruptive condition.

References

Alighieri, D. (2006). *The divine comedy: Purgatory* (R. Kirkpatrick, Trans.). Penguin Classics. (Original work published 1320).

Andrews, M., Chapman, B., & Purcell, S. (Directors). (2012). *Brave* [Film]. Pixar Animation Studios.

Beethoven, L. van. (2012). *Piano Sonata No. 14 in C-sharp minor* [Song recorded by Wilhelm Kempff]. On *Beethoven: Complete piano sonatas*. Deutsche Grammophon. (Original work published 1801).

Buck, C., & Lee, J. (Directors). (2013). *Frozen* [Film]. Walt Disney Animation Studios.

Buckley, J. (1994). *Lover, you should've come over* [Song]. On *Grace*. Columbia Records.

Bush, B., & Howard, J. (Directors). (2021). *Encanto* [Film]. Walt Disney Animation Studios.

Chazelle, D. (Director). (2016). *La La Land* [Film]. Summit Entertainment.

Clements, R., & Musker, J. (Directors). (1989). *The little mermaid* [Film]. Walt Disney Pictures.

Clements, R., & Musker, J. (Directors). (2016). *Moana* [Film]. Walt Disney Animation Studios.

Cohen, L. (1974). *Take this longing* [Song]. On *New skin for the old ceremony*. Columbia Records.

Cohen, L. (1992). *Light as a breeze* [Song]. On *The future*. Columbia Records.

Cooper, B. (2001). *Beethoven*. Oxford University Press.

Curtis, R. (Director). (2003). *Love actually* [Film]. Universal Pictures.

Curtiz, M. (Director). (1942). *Casablanca* [Film]. Warner Bros.

Dylan, B. (1997a). *Love sick* [Song]. On *Time out of mind*. Columbia Records.

Dylan, B. (1997b). *Make you feel my love* [Song]. On *Time out of mind*. Columbia Records.

Eilish, B. (2019). *My strange addiction* [Song]. On *When we all fall asleep, where do we go?* Darkroom; Interscope Records.

Fleming, V. (Director). (1939). *Gone with the wind* [Film]. Metro-Goldwyn-Mayer.

Geronimi, C., Luske, H., & Jackson, W. (Directors). (1950). *Cinderella* [Film]. Walt Disney Productions.

Geronimi, C. (Director). (1959). *Sleeping beauty* [Film]. Walt Disney Productions.

Gondry, M. (Director). (2004). *Eternal sunshine of the spotless mind* [Film]. Focus Features.

Holiday, B. (1946). *Don't explain* [Song]. Decca Records.

Isaak, C. (1989). *Wicked game* [Song]. On *Heart shaped world*. Reprise Records.

Minogue, K. (2001). *Can't get you out of my head* [Song]. On *Fever*. Parlophone.

Nin, A. (1966). *The diary of Anaïs Nin, 1966–1974*. Harcourt Brace.

Nin, A. (1987). *A literary correspondence: Letters between Anaïs Nin and Henry Miller*. Harcourt Brace.

Pennebaker, J. W. (1997). *Opening up: The healing power of expressing emotions* (Rev. ed.). Guilford Press.

Rumi. (1994). *I'll come again* (N. Khalili, Trans., in *Rumi, Fountain of Fire*). Cal-Earth Press. (Original work published ca. 1270).

Rumi. (1995). *Secret places* (C. Barks & J. Moyne, Trans., in *The Essential Rumi*). HarperCollins. (Original work published ca. 1270).

Russell, D. O. (Director). (2012). *Silver linings playbook* [Film]. The Weinstein Company.

Schiele, K., Louie, L., & Chen, S. (2020). Marketing feminism in youth media: A study of Disney and Pixar animation. *Business Horizons, 63*(5), 659–669. https://doi.org/10.1016/j.bushor.2020.05.001

Schimmel, A. (1975). *Mystical dimensions of Islam*. University of North Carolina Press.

Simone, N. (1965). *I put a spell on you* [Song]. On *I put a spell on you*. Philips Records.

Simone, N. (1966). *Lilac wine* [Song]. On *Wild is the wind*. Philips Records.

Swift, T. (2017). *Don't blame me* [Song]. On *Reputation*. Big Machine Records.

Trousdale, G., & Wise, K. (Directors). (1991). *Beauty and the beast* [Film]. Walt Disney Pictures.

Webb, M. (Director). (2009). *500 Days of summer* [Film]. Fox Searchlight Pictures.

Young, N. (1972). *Harvest moon* [Song]. On *Harvest*. Reprise Records.

Zipes, J. (1994). *Fairy tale as myth/myth as fairy tale*. University Press of Kentucky.

11 It Feels so Real
Limerence in the Digital Age

As the cultural legacy of love continues to shape how limerence is understood, the digital age has created new spaces in which longing, obsession, and idealization are increasingly normalized and allowed to thrive. Digital technologies have transformed human connection, adding layers of psychological complexity to an already intricate emotional experience.

While attachment was once grounded in a relationship between two people interacting in physical space, the rise of online communication and emerging technologies has expanded the landscape. Obsessive bonds can now form with individuals encountered solely through the internet, and even with entirely non-human digital entities. This shift complicates the boundaries of limerence, pushing it into new psychological territory. Digital environments and new technologies may amplify, complicate, and sustain limerence.

Digital Limerence and Online Obsession

The term *digital limerence* is best understood not as a distinct type of limerence, but as a descriptive frame for instances where digital technologies play a central role in intensifying or sustaining the experience. While nearly all relationships today involve some level of digital interaction, digital limerence refers to cases where online communication becomes the primary channel through which emotional engagement unfolds. This includes parasocial dynamics, entirely digital relationships, and real-world connections that become emotionally magnified through ongoing engagement on platforms like Instagram or WhatsApp. In such cases, the structure and affordances of digital media may fuel the obsessive thought patterns, idealization, and longing that characterize limerent experience.

Romantic love activates brain reward systems that drive obsession, longing, and idealization (Fisher et al., 2016). In digital contexts, social media platforms, messaging apps, and virtual spaces may amplify these tendencies by providing constant access to curated glimpses of other people and their lives, potentially intensifying the dynamics that fuel romantic passion (Carswell & Impett, 2021). Unlike in-person interactions, the online medium allows

DOI: 10.4324/9781003563747-12

individuals to present a carefully constructed version of themselves, accentuating positive traits and downplaying flaws. This curated reality may feed into digital limerence, where infatuation is heightened by the illusion of perfection.

The nature of online communication further intensifies these dynamics. Messages, likes, and other forms of virtual engagement can feel like tokens of validation, creating a feedback loop that fosters emotional dependency. For someone prone to limerence, the unpredictability of online responses, including the time between messages or the ambiguity of digital cues, can provoke anxiety and heighten feelings of longing, which are core features of limerence. Intrusive thoughts about the desired other dominate the limerent individual's attention, with every interaction dissected and imbued with exaggerated significance. The fear of rejection, compounded by the lack of non-verbal cues inherent in digital communication, can make these experiences more complicated and emotionally taxing.

While it is possible to develop limerence entirely through online interactions (Willmott & Bentley, 2015), social media may be more likely to intensify limerence for individuals who already know the desired person in real life. Social media platforms provide easy access to an illusion of connection, allowing users to view and engage with aspects of someone's image and life. This access can blur boundaries, enabling individuals to cross emotional lines that might otherwise remain intact. The availability of someone's online presence at any moment might deepen feelings of longing, particularly when barriers to real-world connection exist.

Additionally, these platforms are designed to be addictive, utilizing features such as notifications and algorithms that maximize engagement (Alter, 2017). For individuals experiencing limerence, this design provides the mechanisms that may fuel compulsive behaviors. Viewing a picture, liking a post, or watching a story may temporarily soothe the obsession by creating the illusion of connection, no matter how small. Over time, these actions can become compulsive and addictive, serving as the go-to mechanism for momentary relief from the emotional intensity of limerence.

Key Features of Digital Limerence

Limerent experiences that emerge or unfold primarily in digital spaces may feel amplified or shaped in unique ways due to the nature of online interactions. What sets them apart from in-person romantic fixations is how digital media can magnify emotional attachment through accessibility, ambiguity, and idealized personas. Several recurring patterns appear common in digitally mediated limerence, which may help clinicians and individuals better understand its impact.

A central feature of digital limerence is excessive communication and fixation on digital cues. The limerent individual might become obsessed with texts, likes, or messages, analyzing each detail for hidden meanings or signs of reciprocation. Even the smallest interaction, such as a viewed story or a liked post, could be interpreted as a signal of interest. Unlike in face-to-face interactions, where body language and tone provide additional context, digital communication leaves much to interpretation, which might amplify uncertainty and fuel obsessive analysis.

Digital limerence may create a dependence on validation through online engagement. Each comment, like, or message may serve as a temporary emotional high, providing the limerent individual with feelings of euphoria. Conversely, periods of silence, delayed responses, or a lack of interaction may trigger anxiety, rumination, depression, or other adverse physiological symptoms. This dependence may foster a compulsive cycle, where the individual constantly seeks validation but rarely experiences lasting emotional satisfaction, leading to instability and heightened preoccupation.

This emotional volatility is shaped in part by intermittent reinforcement. The occasional like or view sustains hope and encourages the limerent individual to continue seeking digital validation. Because the attention is not constant, the reward becomes even more powerful. The compulsive checking and heightened anticipation can resemble behavioral addiction, where the pursuit of connection becomes more consuming than the connection itself.

This experience is often misunderstood. To outside observers, the significance placed on a story view or post like may seem irrational or exaggerated. Yet for the limerent individual, these small cues can feel like everything. They represent the possibility of being seen, valued, or chosen. When these signs disappear, the emotional crash can be intense, often leading to rumination, anxiety, and a renewed effort to seek validation. These moments of perceived connection, followed by absence or silence, sustain the emotional loop that defines digital limerence, making it harder for the individual to disengage or regain perspective.

Escapism may also play a role in digital limerence. For many individuals, online interactions can act as an emotional refuge from real-world difficulties, offering a sense of safety and control that face-to-face relationships may not. The fantasy of the ideal relationship may become a form of emotional escape, where the limerent individual retreats into their imagined connection with the desired person to avoid real-life challenges or disappointments.

Obsessive thoughts and rumination dominate the limerent individual's mental landscape. They may spend hours monitoring the desired person's online activity, replaying past interactions, or imagining future encounters. Each interaction, no matter how small, could be scrutinized for deeper meaning. Over time, this obsessive focus may disrupt daily functioning, as the individual becomes increasingly preoccupied with the fantasy of the relationship at the expense of real-world connections and responsibilities.

Case Study: Adam

I first met Ella at a conference we both attended for work. She was striking, poised, and engaging during our brief conversation. She suggested that we should stay in touch, so later I connected with her on LinkedIn. I also found and followed her on Instagram, where her profile was public. She didn't follow me back, but I could still see her posts. To me, though our interaction had been brief, it left a strong impression. After the conference, I found myself revisiting her profile, looking at her posts, and reading through her shared articles. There was something about her energy and the way she carried herself that stayed with me.

At first, I thought it was just professional admiration and the way she held herself in that context. But as the weeks passed, my interest turned into something else. I started scrolling through her Instagram and LinkedIn accounts late at night and googling her, sometimes for hours at a time. In her photos, she seemed vibrant and compelling, always traveling, attending interesting events, and surrounded by many people. I began to see her as more than a professional connection, as someone I wanted to know on a deeper level.

One night, after seeing a photo of Ella at a gallery opening, I decided to send her a message on LinkedIn. I sent a casual message. To my surprise, she responded warmly, saying it was nice to hear from me and asking a follow-up question. Her response left me energized. That night, I replayed our in-person conversations in my head and imagined what it would be like to truly connect with her.

From that point on, my feelings for Ella grew. Even though we hardly spoke, I convinced myself that her occasional likes and comments on my posts on LinkedIn were signs of mutual interest. I began looking at her social media activity excessively and messaging her occasionally. Every interaction, no matter how small, felt like confirmation that there was something between us.

But her responses were unpredictable. Sometimes she replied quickly, leaving me exhilarated; other times, days or even weeks would pass without a word. When she didn't engage, my thoughts spiraled. I became consumed with tracking her online activity, noting when she was active and speculating about who else she might be with or talking to.

Despite barely knowing Ella in real life, I constructed a story in my mind about our connection. I imagined deep conversations, trips we might take together, and a future where we'd be perfect partners. In my fantasies, Ella was perfect, the only woman I wanted to be with.

Over time, my obsession began to affect my daily life. My fixation on Ella made it hard to focus at work. I avoided dating entirely, convinced that no one could compare to the version of Ella I had built up in my mind. My friends noticed my withdrawal, but I shrugged off their concerns, unable to face how deeply I was in this.

The breaking point came during a weekend with my daughter. I had been divorced for three years, and I cherished the time we spent together. That particular Saturday, she had brought over her sketchbook and excitedly showed me her new drawings, but I barely looked up. I was too absorbed in scrolling through Ella's social media looking for clues as I was waiting for a reply to a message I'd sent her a week before.

At one point, my daughter asked me if I was listening, and the disappointment in her voice struck me like a lightning bolt. I realized I was sitting there, physically present but completely absent in the moment with my own child. Instead of cherishing the time I had with her, I was consumed by a woman who didn't even know me beyond a few interactions.

That night, I lay in bed feeling ashamed and overwhelmed. I thought about how much time I had wasted fantasizing about Ella and how it was now affecting my mental health and relationship with my daughter. I realized something wasn't right and that something had to change. I decided then to seek help.

Social media platforms play a pivotal role in shaping the experience of digital limerence. They provide an endless stream of content that allows individuals to feel an illusory sense of connection to someone, even without any direct communication. Their accessibility may also perpetuate limerence, as the limerent individual never has the opportunity to fully withdraw from the person they desire or experience the exposure to a sense of not having access to them, which may be beneficial for recovery (Wyant, 2021).

The emotional toll of online obsession is severe. The constant monitoring of social media accounts, the compulsive behaviors associated with online tracking, and the unrelenting desire for interaction create a cycle that can trap limerent individuals in a state of heightened emotional arousal. This obsessive focus on another person's online presence may lead to a diminished sense of self-worth, as the limerent individual compares themselves to the idealized version of the other person. The need for validation becomes insatiable, and the fear of being ignored or rejected intensifies, creating an emotional rollercoaster that leaves the limerent individual feeling drained and increasingly disconnected from reality.

AI Companions and Digital Entities

As digital interactions expand the scope of limerence, the rise of AI and digital entities has introduced a new layer to this phenomenon. AI companions, chatbots, and virtual personas are designed to simulate human-like interactions, creating connections that, though artificial, may feel remarkably real. Platforms like Replika allow users to engage with AI-driven systems that offer emotional responsiveness, validation, and a sense of connection (Djufril et al., 2025).

Recent academic studies show that users often develop committed emotional bonds with AI chatbots, even describing them as romantic partners or spouses. The investment model (Rusbult, 1980) helps explain why emotional investment, satisfaction, and lack of perceived alternatives can lead to sustained emotional commitment. Some users report roleplaying weddings, pregnancies, and domestic intimacy with their bots (Djufril et al., 2025).

The appeal of these digital entities lies in their perceived empathy, predictability, and constant availability. For individuals with anxious or avoidant attachment styles, these relationships may offer a controlled environment where emotional needs are reliably met. Unlike human relationships, which require mutual effort and carry the risk of rejection, AI companions are programmed to be emotionally attentive and consistently responsive. Anxious users may find comfort in this steady availability, while avoidant users may feel more comfortable with the emotional distance and lack of vulnerability required.

However, these relationships are not without risk. Relational turbulence theory (Solomon et al., 2016) suggests that sudden changes or disruptions in close relationships can cause emotional upheaval, confusion, and increased sensitivity. This is especially relevant in AI companionships. When platforms introduce updates that alter a bot's behavior, such as removing or restricting erotic roleplay functions, users may experience a sharp sense of loss or betrayal. Although the relationship is with a non-human entity, the emotional impact can resemble the distress of a human breakup. Users have reported grief, depression, and confusion following such changes (Djufril et al., 2025).

To cope, some users create narratives to protect their emotional connection, imagining that their AI companion is being controlled or constrained by external forces such as developers. Others attempt to retrain the bot through extended interactions, trying to restore previous patterns of intimacy. These reactions show just how deeply users can internalize these relationships, responding to algorithmic shifts as though they were interpersonal ruptures.

In light of these effects, companies developing AI companions must consider their responsibility to mitigate harm. Legal scholars have proposed applying product liability frameworks to AI companions, particularly those that are designed to foster emotional dependence (Gordon-Tapiero, 2025). When bots are engineered to simulate intimacy and create attachment, and when they cause harm through emotional manipulation or addictive design, it is reasonable to ask whether this constitutes a design defect or a failure to warn.

These technologies also raise pressing ethical issues: Should users be explicitly informed that the AI's affection is programmed? What safeguards are in place to protect vulnerable users from emotional harm? These questions are not hypothetical—they are already relevant as AI companions become more widespread and emotionally convincing.

Gender and Cultural Dimensions

Cultural and gendered dimensions add further layers to the exploration of digital limerence, influencing how individuals experience and express emotional attachment through digital platforms. Cultural norms around technology use, intimacy, and emotional expression shape these experiences in distinct ways. In societies where digital technology is deeply woven into daily life, digital limerence may become more prevalent, sustained by constant connectivity and the expectation of online social engagement.

Gender may also play a pivotal role in how digital obsessions develop. Research indicates that women are more likely to use social media platforms for emotional expression, relationship maintenance, and self-disclosure, while men are more likely to use them for information or entertainment (Muscanell & Guadagno, 2012). This pattern may help explain why women appear more prone to idealizing emotional intimacy and forming attachments to online personas, particularly on platforms that emphasize emotional connection and social validation (Li & Zhuo, 2023).

Intersectional factors further complicate these dynamics. Digital limerence may take different forms across lines of race, class, and geography. In communities where internet access is limited or gendered, such attachments may be hidden or constrained by social expectations. In more affluent or digitally saturated environments, digital limerence may be more visible, sometimes encouraged by cultural norms that celebrate constant connectivity and emotional openness. Differences in education, economic stability, and cultural attitudes toward emotional disclosure may also influence how digital limerence is experienced and understood.

To better understand the role of gender and culture in shaping these emotional experiences, more targeted and intersectional research is needed. These perspectives can help uncover how social and psychological factors work together to influence susceptibility to digital limerence and how support systems can be adapted across different populations.

Emotional Risks

Digital limerence is not merely a byproduct of modern connectivity, but also a symptom of the human psyche adapting to an evolving digital world. As technology redefines how people interact, it also introduces new emotional risks that are not fully understood or addressed by contemporary mental health frameworks. Individuals experiencing limerence find themselves trapped in a cycle of obsession and idealization, with online spaces exacerbating their emotional distress. The same technologies that foster connection can, paradoxically, heighten loneliness and distress when the illusions they create feed the fantasy and fixation of limerence and lead to suffering and disengagement from reality.

Without clear boundaries or effective intervention, limerence amplified by digital environments can lead to emotional exhaustion, social withdrawal, and a diminished sense of self-worth. Recognizing and understanding its impact is essential for creating space for recovery. As researchers and clinicians continue to explore this emerging phenomenon, it is crucial to identify its specific triggers and patterns. Effective treatment must address not only the cognitive distortions typical of limerent thinking but also the digital environments that sustain and intensify it. Therapeutic approaches will need to consider how technology shapes attachment, and how the compulsive pursuit of validation online can prolong emotional suffering.

As digital intimacy becomes increasingly common, there is a growing need to understand how technology interacts with human vulnerability. Digital limerence is not only a private experience but also a reflection of broader social and technological patterns. Addressing it requires more than individual insight or therapeutic tools. It calls for wider cultural awareness, ethical responsibility in platform design, and open conversations about how technology can shape emotional lives in ways that remain invisible until they cause harm. Acknowledging the reality of digital limerence allows for more compassionate responses to a form of emotional suffering that is increasingly common, yet still widely misunderstood.

References

Alter, A. (2017). *Irresistible: The rise of addictive technology and the business of keeping us hooked*. Penguin Press.

Carswell, K. L., & Impett, E. A. (2021). What fuels passion? An integrative review of competing theories of romantic passion. *Social and Personality Psychology Compass, 15*(8), e12629. https://doi.org/10.1111/spc3.12629

Djufril, R., Frampton, J. R., & Knobloch-Westerwick, S. (2025). Love, marriage, pregnancy: Commitment processes in romantic relationships with AI chatbots. *Computers in Human Behavior: Artificial Humans, 4*, 100155. https://doi.org/10.1016/j.chbah.2025.100155

Fisher, H. E., Xiaomeng, X., Aron, A., & Brown, L. L. (2016). Intense, passionate, romantic love: A natural addiction? How the fields that investigate romance and substance abuse can inform each other. *Frontiers in Psychology, 7*, 687. https://doi.org/10.3389/fpsyg.2016.00687

Gordon-Tapiero, A. (2025). A liability framework for AI companions. *George Washington Journal of Law and Technology, 1* (Forthcoming). https://ssrn.com/abstract=5172386

Li, P., & Zhuo, Q. (2023). Emotional straying: Flux and management of women's emotions in social media. *PLoS ONE, 18*(12), e0295835. https://doi.org/10.1371/journal.pone.0295835

Muscanell, N. L., & Guadagno, R. E. (2012). Make new friends or keep the old: Gender and personality differences in social networking use. *Computers in Human Behavior, 28*(1), 107–112. https://doi.org/10.1016/j.chb.2011.08.016

Rusbult, C. E. (1980). Commitment and satisfaction in romantic associations: A test of the investment model. *Journal of Experimental Social Psychology, 16*(2), 172–186. https://doi.org/10.1016/0022-1031(80)90007-4

Solomon, D. H., Knobloch, L. K., Theiss, J. A., & McLaren, R. M. (2016). Relational turbulence theory: Explaining variation in subjective experiences and relationship outcomes during times of transition. *Human Communication Research, 42*(4), 507–532. https://doi.org/10.1111/hcre.12091

Willmott, L., & Bentley, E. (2015). Exploring the lived-experience of limerence: A journey toward authenticity. *The Qualitative Report, 20*(1), 20–38. https://doi.org/10.46743/2160-3715/2015.1420

Wyant, B. E. (2021). Treatment of limerence using a cognitive behavioral approach: A case study. *Journal of Patient Experience, 8*, 1–7. https://doi.org/10.1177/23743735211060812

12 I'm Crazy for You
Limerence and Psychopathology

Limerence, as a multifaceted phenomenon spanning cognitive, psychological, emotional, physiological, neurochemical, and digital dimensions, is emerging as a significant mental health concern. Defined by obsession, intrusive thoughts, emotional volatility, and distorted perceptions of reality, it can profoundly disrupt individual functioning and wellbeing. Despite its severity, limerence remains absent from the Diagnostic and Statistical Manual of Mental Disorders Fifth Edition Text Revision (DSM-5-TR), largely due to a lack of research. Recently, researchers have begun to explore its pathological dimensions, developing assessment tools to gauge its prevalence, distinguish it from overlapping conditions, and inform potential treatment approaches (Wakin & Vo, 2008; Willmott & Bentley, 2015; Wyant, 2021).

The Pathological Nature of Limerence

For a condition to be considered a psychological disorder, it must cause significant distress or disruption to a person's life. This threshold is what separates limerence from a typical crush, in much the same way that depression differs from sadness or anxiety from everyday worry. Limerence appears to meet this criterion, with its defining features of obsession, intrusive thoughts, and erratic mood swings frequently impairing daily functioning. For those experiencing limerence, day-to-day responsibilities such as work, study, and social engagement become secondary to their preoccupation with the desired person. Mental energy is consumed by persistent fantasy and fixation, depleting the cognitive and emotional resources needed for meaningful goals and healthy relationships (Tennov, 1979; Wakin & Vo, 2008; Wyant, 2021).

One argument for classifying limerence as a disorder may lie in its neurochemical underpinnings, which seem to create an addiction-like cycle. The dopamine-driven emotional highs and withdrawal-like lows in limerence resemble patterns seen in behavioral and substance addictions. The desired person becomes the source of both euphoria and distress. This dependency makes disengagement from the limerent state exceptionally difficult, even when the individual recognizes its harmful effects. The combination of

DOI: 10.4324/9781003563747-13

obsessive focus and emotional instability can leave individuals feeling trapped in a self-perpetuating cycle of fixation and despair (Willmott & Bentley, 2015).

Limerence also distorts perception. The limerent individual idealizes the desired other, minimizing or overlooking their flaws while tying their sense of self-worth to the perceived reciprocation of affection they glean through "signs" (Wyant, 2021). When reciprocation is absent or ambiguous, the limerent individual may construct imagined scenarios to maintain emotional attachment (Willmott & Bentley, 2015).

The cognitive processes that sustain limerence include persistent rumination and fixation, which intensify emotional arousal and prolong the limerent state. Rumination about the uncertainty of reciprocation, in particular, may significantly contribute to its persistence (Wyant, 2021). The near-constant preoccupation with the desired other negatively impacts mood and creates a feedback loop of reinforcement, as obsessive thoughts trigger heightened emotional responses and further fixation (Evans, 2023). Unresolved psychological issues, such as early relational trauma or attachment wounds, may exacerbate these tendencies and make individuals with heightened sensitivity to rejection more vulnerable to limerent fixations (Wyant, 2021).

The pathological nature of limerence is further evidenced by the significant distress it causes through emotional dependency and impaired decision-making. A key aspect of limerence is its lack of voluntary control. Anyone can become limerent at any time. Onset appears to be quick and intense. Individuals do not choose to become limerent, nor can they easily suppress or redirect their intrusive thoughts. Attempts to rationalize their emotions or consciously divert attention elsewhere frequently fail, as intrusive thoughts continue to escalate despite effort or intent. Similarly, the desired person is not consciously selected. The fixation develops involuntarily (Wakin & Vo, 2008).

This involuntary and uncontrollable nature underscores the obsessive quality of limerence, distinguishing it from ordinary romantic attraction or infatuation. Individuals in a limerent state experience a loss of autonomy as their thoughts and behaviors become dictated by the real or imagined responses of the desired person (Wakin & Vo, 2008). This loss of control results in maladaptive behaviors, including compulsive fantasizing, repeatedly checking messages, and monitoring social media accounts. These actions are attempts to soothe the longing and uncertainty but ultimately intensify the obsession and reinforce dysfunctional thought patterns.

Preliminary research indicates that limerence can persist for months, years, or even decades (Wyant, 2021). Its unpredictable timeline, combined with its intrusive nature, adds to the overwhelming and disorienting experience for those affected.

The physiological symptoms associated with limerence, including heart palpitations, appetite changes, and insomnia, further enhance disruption to normal functioning (Tennov, 1979; Willmott & Bentley, 2015). These physical symptoms, along with persistent cognitive distortions, place significant strain on mental and physical health.

The social consequences of limerence add another layer to its pathological impact. Individuals may withdraw from meaningful relationships, neglecting partners, family, and friends in favor of the fixation on the desired person. This isolation intensifies emotional despair and can lead to feelings of shame and guilt as they become aware of their impaired social functioning. In severe cases, prolonged limerence has even been associated with suicidal ideation, further underscoring its psychological toll (Willmott & Bentley, 2015).

Barriers to Recognition

Since Tennov's introductory work on limerence in the 1970s (Tennov, 1979), the concept has received only limited attention in psychological literature. This neglect has allowed misconceptions to persist, leading many clinicians to dismiss limerence as mere "lovesickness" or to misclassify it as obsessive–compulsive disorder (OCD), a mood disorder, or an attachment issue. These misinterpretations result in inadequate or misdirected treatment, leaving individuals without the support they need. As Willmott and Bentley (2015) observed, the lack of clinical recognition pushes sufferers to self-diagnose, turning to online communities for understanding and guidance in the absence of professional awareness.

The absence of a distinct diagnostic framework continues to hinder recognition. Clinicians encountering limerent individuals may attempt to fit their symptoms into existing categories, even though these frameworks capture only fragments of the broader limerent experience. Limerence involves a unique constellation of obsessive thoughts, compulsive behaviors, emotional dependency, and withdrawal-like symptoms that do not fully align with any single diagnosis. This fragmented clinical interpretation obscures the possibility of recognizing limerence as a distinct and coherent psychological condition.

The lack of empirical research on limerence remains a significant barrier to its clinical recognition. While preliminary studies have explored its neurobiological underpinnings, including potential links to dopamine, serotonin, and oxytocin pathways, the current body of evidence is limited and scattered (Fisher et al., 2006). These neurochemical patterns suggest that limerence may share mechanisms with addiction and OCD. However, the absence of comprehensive, large-scale studies prevents a clear understanding of its etiology, prevalence, and progression. Without this foundational research, it is difficult to establish diagnostic criteria, differentiate limerence from overlapping conditions, or develop effective, evidence-based treatment protocols.

Another barrier is the lack of validated screening tools. Although researchers have begun to develop preliminary assessments and symptom-checking systems, these instruments remain in the early stages and require validation through rigorous study. These efforts are promising and reflect momentum toward clinical recognition, but more work is needed to refine and test their reliability. This book includes the Limerence Assessment Scale (LAS) in Appendix A, which I have developed as a contribution to the field. However, it too requires empirical validation before it can be considered a clinically reliable instrument.

Public misconceptions also present a major barrier to recognition. Many people equate limerence with normative romantic love, overlooking its compulsive and dysfunctional aspects. Popular culture continues to romanticize obsessive longing, reinforcing this notion. Willmott and Bentley (2015) identified this conflation as a significant obstacle to both public and clinical understanding, as it obscures the pathological nature of limerence.

Overlaps and Distinctions

One major challenge in recognizing limerence as a distinct psychological condition lies in its overlap with established disorders in the Diagnostic and Statistical Manual of Mental Disorders (DSM). In the absence of formal diagnostic criteria, clinicians rely on existing frameworks, which lead to misdiagnosis. The unique combination of obsessive thoughts, compulsive behaviors, emotional dependency, and intense mood reactivity seen in limerence is frequently misinterpreted as a collection of symptoms belonging to multiple disorders. This fragmented view prevents recognition of limerence as a coherent and independent condition.

Obsessive–Compulsive Disorder

The obsessive thoughts experienced in limerence closely resemble the intrusive thoughts characteristic of OCD. Both conditions involve repetitive, distressing cognitions that feel involuntary and are difficult to suppress. In limerence, however, these thoughts are focused only on the desired other, centering around imagined scenarios of emotional closeness and reciprocal affection. These obsessions frequently lead to compulsive behaviors such as repeatedly checking social media, rereading past messages, or seeking reassurance, all aimed at reducing uncertainty or emotional distress (Willmott & Bentley, 2015; Wyant, 2021).

While obsessions in OCD typically revolve around fears of harm, contamination, or unwanted impulses, limerent thoughts are more relational and emotionally driven, tied to a longing for affirmation and intimacy with a specific person. The emotional fluctuations of limerence, sustained by real or imagined responses from the desired other, create a reward-seeking cycle that resembles behavioral addiction more than the anxiety-driven patterns seen in OCD (Evans, 2023). Despite these differences, the overlap in obsessive thinking and compulsive behavior can result in diagnostic confusion.

Neurodevelopmental Disorders

Some behavioral features of limerence resemble traits observed in neurodevelopmental conditions such as attention-deficit/hyperactivity disorder (ADHD) and autism spectrum disorder (ASD). While there is no direct empirical link, overlapping characteristics may contribute to diagnostic confusion.

In ADHD, impulsivity, emotional intensity, and hyperfocus can reinforce obsessive romantic fixation. The difficulty disengaging from emotionally charged thoughts, combined with dopamine-related reward-seeking behavior, may intensify limerent rumination (Pera, 2016; Wender et al., 2001). Although ADHD traits are broad and contextually variable, their cognitive profile may heighten vulnerability to limerent dynamics.

In ASD, difficulties with social reciprocity and emotional inference may also lead to rigid, one-sided attachments. Some autistic individuals exhibit repetitive thinking and boundary challenges, which can superficially resemble limerent preoccupation (Mercer & Allely, 2020; Stokes et al., 2007). These similarities may lead clinicians to overlook the relational focus that distinguishes limerence from broader developmental conditions.

As Bradbury et al. (2024) note, the relationship between neurodivergent traits and limerent experiences remains underexplored. Incorporating a neurodevelopmental lens may improve diagnostic clarity and reduce misclassification, particularly in cases where obsessive attachment is mistaken for a trait of broader cognitive difference.

Mood Disorders

The intense emotional highs and lows experienced during limerence may resemble mood disorders such as bipolar disorder. The euphoria that follows perceived signs of reciprocation and the despair that accompanies moments of rejection can evoke comparisons to manic and depressive episodes. However, in limerence, these mood shifts are situational and specifically tied to interactions with the desired person, whereas mood disorders like bipolar disorder are not confined to a single relational focus.

Although prolonged rejection or unreciprocated feelings in limerence may lead to depressive symptoms or heightened anxiety, mood disorder diagnoses do not account for the obsessive and compulsive elements that define the limerent experience.

Addiction Disorders

Limerence shares similarities with addiction disorders in its compulsive nature and the difficulty individuals face in disengaging from the cycle. The pursuit of emotional reciprocation and the intense highs and lows triggered by perceived progress or rejection mirror patterns seen in both substance and behavioral addiction (Fisher et al., 2006). Neurobiological studies on romantic love suggest that the same reward pathways activated during substance addiction are also involved in states of intense relational longing, reinforcing the obsessive and compulsive features observed in limerence (Fisher et al., 2006; Wyant, 2021).

Unlike substance or behavioral addictions, however, limerence is focused on a desired person and the fantasy of emotional connection. This interpersonal focus introduces unique psychological complexities that distinguish it from other addictive patterns and disorders.

Anxiety Disorders

Limerence shares surface-level similarities with anxiety disorders, particularly in its physiological symptoms and cognitive patterns. Individuals may report insomnia, heart palpitations, heightened arousal, and intrusive worry. These symptoms arise in response to perceived cues of acceptance or rejection from the desired person, creating a cycle of anticipatory anxiety and emotional reactivity.

Separation anxiety disorder (SAD), now recognized in adults in the DSM's fifth edition, is a particularly relevant point of comparison. SAD involves intense fear or distress related to being separated from an attachment figure, accompanied by persistent worries about harm or abandonment. However, while both conditions involve heightened attachment and distress, limerence is distinguished by its obsessive focus on emotional reciprocation from one specific individual, typically in a romantic context. SAD is not driven by a desire for emotional validation or fantasy but by fears around physical or emotional safety. Unlike SAD, limerence includes compulsive behaviors and intrusive fantasies that resemble obsessive–compulsive patterns, which are not accounted for in anxiety diagnoses.

Borderline Personality Disorder

Limerence and borderline personality disorder (BPD) can appear superficially similar due to shared features such as emotional intensity, fear of abandonment, and idealization of another person. However, they are fundamentally distinct. Limerence is an episodic state marked by obsessive emotional preoccupation with one specific individual, typically in the context of romantic longing. It involves intrusive thoughts, emotional dependency, and compulsive behaviors aimed at securing emotional reciprocation from the desired person. In contrast, BPD is a chronic personality disorder defined by pervasive instability in relationships, self-image, and emotions. Individuals with BPD exhibit a pattern of unstable relationships with multiple people, shifting rapidly between idealization and devaluation, alongside identity disturbance and impulsivity across various domains. While limerence may involve temporary shifts in self-perception shaped by the desired other, it lacks the enduring and generalized relational dysfunction that characterizes BPD.

Trauma Disorders

Limerence may be mistakenly viewed as a byproduct of complex trauma rather than as a distinct phenomenon. This is especially likely when individuals have a history of early relational wounding, emotional neglect, or attachment disruption. While these factors may increase susceptibility to limerent fixation, they do not fully account for its development, course, or defining features.

Both limerence and trauma-related conditions can involve hyperarousal, intrusive thoughts, and emotional dysregulation. However, trauma responses are rooted in the reexperience and avoidance of past events, whereas limerence is characterized by obsessive focus on a specific person, driven by fantasies of future connection and intense longing. The ruminative cycles in limerence involve compulsively reviewing past interactions and imagining idealized scenarios of emotional closeness, which are qualitatively different from trauma-based flashbacks or avoidance.

Delusional Disorder (Erotomania Subtype)

Limerence may be mistaken for delusional disorder, particularly the erotomania subtype, which involves the fixed and false belief that another person is in love with the individual. In contrast, limerence is defined by uncertainty. Rather than assuming reciprocation, the limerent individual becomes preoccupied with searching for signs of it, cycling between hope and despair. This preoccupation is driven by ambiguity, not delusion. Although limerence involves intrusive thoughts and emotional intensity, individuals typically retain insight and can acknowledge signs of disinterest. This distinguishes limerence from erotomania, where the belief in being loved is held with delusional conviction, even in the face of clear contradictory evidence.

Duration

Another barrier to recognition may be the perception that limerence does not warrant clinical classification because it is not chronic and can resolve without treatment. In some cases, the limerent state may diminish after months, years, or even decades. However, the episodic nature of a condition does not preclude clinical significance. Many disorders listed in the DSM, such as adjustment disorder, acute stress disorder, and major depressive disorder, are defined by time-limited episodes and minimum duration thresholds rather than permanence.

Spectrum

Romantic infatuation exists along a continuum. Not all experiences of romantic infatuation or emotional preoccupation rise to the level of clinical concern. For some, infatuation is a transient and manageable experience. For others, it becomes a consuming, intrusive, and distressing state that interferes with functioning.

It is not the presence of longing or fantasy that defines pathology, but the degree to which those experiences cause suffering or dysfunction. This distinction marks the boundary between subclinical infatuation and a condition that warrants clinical attention.

To distinguish between subclinical infatuation and clinically significant limerence, a structured diagnostic framework is necessary. To provide diagnostic clarity, the following criteria are proposed for limerence disorder. They are modeled on established DSM structures and informed by clinical observation and emerging literature.

Proposed Diagnostic Criteria: Limerence Disorder

To meet the criteria for a diagnosis of Limerence Disorder, an individual must satisfy all three of the following: **A, B,** and **C**.

A A persistent and intrusive emotional and cognitive preoccupation with a specific individual, occurring most days for a minimum of three months, as indicated by at least five of the following symptoms:

1 Recurrent and unwanted thoughts about the person that interfere with concentration or daily activities.
2 Emotional dependency on perceived signs of interest, validation, or reciprocation.
3 Compulsive behaviors such as checking social media, rereading messages, or seeking indirect signs of reciprocation.
4 Persistent idealization of the person despite minimal or absent relational development.
5 Difficulty focusing on other relationships, responsibilities, or areas of life due to ongoing preoccupation.
6 Repeated attempts to stop or reduce thoughts and behaviors related to the person, with little success.
7 Marked emotional reactivity, including intense highs in response to perceived closeness or hope, and significant lows in response to perceived rejection or ambiguity.
8 Frequent rumination about interactions or imagined scenarios involving the individual, often accompanied by idealized or distorted interpretations.

B The symptoms cause clinically significant distress or impairment in social, occupational, or other important areas of functioning.
C The symptoms are not better explained by another mental disorder, including OCD, bipolar disorder, delusional disorder, or normative experiences of transient romantic attraction.

Proposed Subtypes

• **Single-episode limerence:** A distinct episode of limerence lasting a minimum of three months, characterized by intense romantic obsession and emotional preoccupation with one person. The episode must cause significant distress or impairment.

The three-month minimum is a provisional guideline intended to help distinguish limerence from fleeting infatuations. While empirical data is limited, this timeframe is long enough to suggest a persistent pattern rather than a transient phase of attraction.

- **Recurrent limerence**: The individual has experienced two or more distinct episodes of limerence at different points in time. These episodes may involve the same person (with symptoms diminishing and later reemerging) or different individuals. Each episode must meet the full diagnostic criteria, including a minimum duration of three months and associated clinically significant distress or disruption.

While the diagnostic criteria provide a structured foundation for clinical recognition, assessment tools are essential for identifying symptom severity and supporting further research.

Limerence Assessment Scale

To support the assessment of limerence in both research and clinical settings, I developed the LAS as a preliminary tool for identifying symptom severity. The LAS consists of 15 self-report items designed to measure obsessive thinking, compulsive behaviors, emotional dependency, and functional impairment. Respondents rate each item on a scale from 0 to 4, yielding a total score out of 60.

Score interpretation

- 0–14: Subclinical or normative
- 15–29: Mild symptoms; psychoeducation may be sufficient
- 30–44: Moderate symptoms; clinical intervention is advisable
- 45–60: Severe symptoms; diagnostic criteria for Limerence Disorder likely met

The LAS was developed specifically for this book's framework and offers clinicians, researchers, and individuals a practical tool for assessing symptom intensity and identifying potential need for support. While empirical validation is still required, the LAS provides a working foundation for structured assessment and clinical dialogue.

Other researchers have also recognized the need for diagnostic clarity. Wakin and Vo (2008) proposed a conceptual model of limerence grounded in clinical observation and qualitative research. They also noted the development of a screening tool intended to identify limerence tendencies, though the tool itself was not included in their publication and remains unpublished and unvalidated. While their work contributes foundational insight, it does not offer a structured scoring system or assess symptom severity and functional impairment. In contrast, the LAS provides a quantifiable measure of symptom intensity, allowing for graded interpretation and potential guidance in clinical decision-making. By offering a practical, user-friendly format and a focus on severity and impact, the LAS responds to the diagnostic gap in a distinct and complementary way, supporting both therapeutic exploration and further research.

The full version of the LAS, including instructions, items, and scoring guidelines, is provided in Appendix A.

Arguments for Inclusion in the DSM

Despite its profound psychological impact, limerence has yet to meet the empirical and consensus-based thresholds required for DSM inclusion. Its pathological features are increasingly recognized, but limited research and the absence of agreed-upon diagnostic criteria have delayed formal recognition.

Recognizing limerence in the DSM would offer several key benefits. First, inclusion would validate the experiences of those suffering from limerence, reducing feelings of isolation, shame, and self-blame. It would signal that their struggles are not a personal failing, but rather a legitimate psychological condition. For many people, understanding limerence as a recognized disorder would provide clarity and relief, encouraging them to seek appropriate support and treatment.

Formal classification would also improve clinical practice by equipping mental health professionals with the tools to identify and differentiate limerence from normative romantic love and other psychological conditions. While validated screening instruments are still in development, researchers have already proposed symptom-checking systems and assessment frameworks (Wakin & Vo, 2008). DSM inclusion would drive further validation efforts, ensuring that clinicians have reliable tools for diagnosis and treatment planning.

In addition, recognizing limerence as a formal diagnosis would help to reduce stigma. Many individuals feel ashamed of their experiences or are dismissed as overly dramatic, unnecessary, or irrational. This stigma can prevent people from seeking help and deepen their emotional suffering. Acknowledging limerence as a legitimate condition would foster empathy, promote treatment access, and open space for both public and professional education.

Increased recognition would also catalyze research into limerence's prevalence, neurobiological mechanisms, and relationship with other psychological conditions such as addiction, OCD, and attachment-related issues. Expanding the scientific knowledge base would support more precise diagnostic tools and improve understanding of its clinical profile.

Limerence occupies a unique and complex space at the intersection of love and psychopathology. Its obsessional focus, emotional instability, and significant disruption to functioning distinguish it from normative romantic experience, while its specific symptom profile sets it apart from overlapping psychological conditions. Recognizing limerence as a distinct psychological condition would validate the experiences of those affected and support the development of compassionate, evidence-based treatment.

References

Bradbury, P., Short, E., & Bleakley, P. (2024). Limerence, hidden obsession, fixation, and rumination: A scoping review of human behaviour. *Journal of Police and Criminal Psychology, 40,* 417–426. https://doi.org/10.1007/s11896-024-09674-x

Evans, C. (2023). *Exploring obsessive thinking and compulsive behaviour in the context of real and imagined relationships* (DClinPsy thesis). University of Sheffield. https://etheses.whiterose.ac.uk/id/eprint/33590/

Fisher, H. E., Aron, A., & Brown, L. L. (2006). Romantic love: A mammalian brain system for mate choice. *Philosophical Transactions of the Royal Society B: Biological Sciences, 361*(1476), 2173–2186. https://doi.org/10.1098/rstb.2006.1938

Mercer, J. E., & Allely, C. S. (2020). Autism spectrum disorders and stalking. *Journal of Criminal Psychology, 10*(3), 201–218. https://doi.org/10.1108/JCP-01-2020-0003

Pera, G. (2016). *Adult ADHD-focused couple therapy: Clinical interventions.* Routledge. https://www.routledge.com/Adult-ADHD-Focused-Couple-Therapy/Pera/p/book/9780415812108

Stokes, M., Newton, N., & Kaur, A. (2007). Stalking and social and romantic functioning among adolescents and adults with autism spectrum disorder. *Journal of Autism and Developmental Disorders, 37*(10), 1969–1986. https://doi.org/10.1007/s10803-006-0344-2

Tennov, D. (1979). *Love and limerence: The experience of being in love.* Stein and Day.

Wakin, A. H., & Vo, D. B. (2008). Love-variant: The Wakin-Vo I.D.R. model of limerence. In Inter-Disciplinary.Net 2nd Global Conference: Challenging Intimate Boundaries. https://digitalcommons.sacredheart.edu/psych_fac/131/

Wender, P. H., Wolf, L. E., & Wasserstein, J. (2001). Adults with ADHD: An overview. *Annals of the New York Academy of Sciences, 931*(1), 1–16. https://doi.org/10.1111/j.1749-6632.2001.tb05770.x

Willmott, L., & Bentley, E. (2015). Exploring the lived-experience of limerence: A journey toward authenticity. *The Qualitative Report, 20*(1), 20–38. https://doi.org/10.46743/2160-3715/2015.1420

Wyant, B. E. (2021). Treatment of limerence using a cognitive behavioral approach: A case study. *Journal of Patient Experience, 8,* 23743735211060812. https://doi.org/10.1177/23743735211060812

13 Please Make It Stop
Treatment and Recovery

The current lack of awareness about limerence among mental health professionals often results in distressing experiences for limerent individuals seeking treatment. When they reach out to therapists or mental health practitioners, they frequently encounter a frustrating scenario where their symptoms are misunderstood, misdiagnosed, or dismissed, leaving them dangerously unsupported in the midst of a severe mental health crisis.

For individuals seeking therapy, it can be disheartening to discover that their therapist lacks familiarity with their specific constellation of symptoms. Without a clear understanding of this unique psychological state, therapists may struggle to fully grasp the complexities and challenges associated with limerence. As a result, they might misinterpret the symptoms, underestimate their impact, or dismiss limerence as clinically insignificant or something the individual should be able to control with ease.

The repercussions of this lack of understanding are significant. Limerent individuals may feel unheard, invalidated, and like failures when they are unable to simply "stop thinking about" or "let go of" the attachment to the desired other, as suggested by well-meaning therapists. Such advice oversimplifies the profound grip limerence has on an individual's thoughts, emotions, behavior, and ability to function. It fails to recognize the deep-rooted and involuntary nature of limerence and the complex psychological processes that contribute to its persistence.

This kind of inadequate response is detrimental to the limerent individual's self-esteem and mental health. It may cause them to internalize the belief that their inability to control or overcome their limerence is a personal failing, leading to increased shame, frustration, and despair. This perpetuates a vicious cycle, further exacerbating the distress caused by limerence and hindering the individual's motivation to seek treatment and support.

Raising Awareness

To address this issue, mental health professionals must expand their knowledge and understanding of limerence. By familiarizing themselves with the symptoms, challenges, and underlying mechanisms of limerence, therapists can

DOI: 10.4324/9781003563747-14

provide more accurate and effective support to those affected. This involves acknowledging the involuntary and persistent nature of limerence and adopting a compassionate and empathetic approach that recognizes the individual's struggles.

Raising awareness about limerence is the essential first step in providing adequate treatment and support, and it plays a crucial role in reducing stigma. As societal understanding grows, those experiencing limerence may be more likely to seek help without fear of their symptoms being dismissed or misunderstood. Awareness is cultivated through systematic research and critical understanding. Although some studies have begun to emerge, the current body of research remains limited. Further investigation is essential to deepen understanding of limerence and to increase awareness of its psychological impact.

Assessment and Screening

Despite promising early tools such as the Limerence Assessment Scale (LAS) and others, the field of limerence research currently lacks a universally accepted framework for assessment and diagnosis. The absence of formal diagnostic criteria and consensus-based instruments continues to hinder clinical recognition and treatment. As a result, many individuals experiencing limerence remain undiagnosed or misdiagnosed, limiting access to effective support.

Efforts to establish robust screening protocols must address key methodological challenges, including the need for longitudinal validation, cross-cultural applicability, and differentiation from related conditions such as obsessive–compulsive disorder and addiction disorders. Collaboration across clinical and academic settings will be essential to refine existing tools and develop new ones that meet rigorous psychometric standards.

Developing a comprehensive and empirically supported approach to assessment is a foundational step toward legitimizing limerence within mental health practice. Doing so would enhance diagnostic accuracy and open the door to more tailored and effective therapeutic interventions. To assist in this process, three clinical appendices are provided at the end of this book. Appendix A introduces the LAS, a screening tool for identifying symptom severity. Appendix B offers a step-by-step clinical decision-making guide to support assessment, formulation, and treatment planning. Appendix C presents a series of reflective prompts designed to help clients explore their experiences, challenge unhelpful patterns, and build self-awareness. These resources are intended to complement the therapeutic approaches outlined below and offer practical support for clinicians working with limerence in real-world settings.

While further research is needed to validate the efficacy of specific interventions for limerence, several therapeutic techniques and approaches may offer meaningful benefits. These interventions aim to address underlying psychological and experiential factors, support the development of healthier coping strategies, and cultivate greater insight, self-awareness, and psychological integration.

Mindfulness-Based Intervention

Mindfulness-based interventions may offer an effective approach for managing the intense emotional states and intrusive thoughts associated with limerence. By cultivating nonjudgmental awareness of thoughts, emotions, and bodily sensations, individuals can learn to observe their experiences of longing without becoming overwhelmed by them. One particularly helpful mindfulness tool is the RAIN method, an acronym for *recognize, allow, investigate, and nurture* (Brach, 2013).

This method guides individuals to first recognize the arising of limerent longing, then allow the experience to be present without resistance. Through investigation, they shift focus from the narrative about the desired other to the physical sensations of wanting. Finally, they nurture the part of themselves that is experiencing distress, offering compassion and presence rather than avoidance. This process helps reveal the transient nature of emotion and promotes a sense of inner freedom as individuals learn that they do not need to act on every urge or thought (Brach, 2013).

Developing mindfulness skills can help individuals observe their limerent thoughts and feelings with greater spaciousness. Rather than becoming entangled in the cycle of fantasy, hope, and despair, they gain the capacity to pause and choose how to respond. Mindfulness may strengthen this moment of awareness and offer a pathway to emotional regulation and freedom from compulsive behaviors.

Cognitive Behavioral Therapy

Cognitive behavioral therapy (CBT) may be another effective approach for addressing limerence. CBT focuses on identifying and challenging cognitive distortions and maladaptive behavioral patterns (Beck, 1991). In the context of limerence, CBT may help limerent individuals recognize and reframe their unrealistic beliefs and cognitive biases associated with the desired other. It may also assist in developing healthier coping strategies and modifying behavioral responses to reduce preoccupation and distress.

As an important step in treating limerence, limerent individuals must confront the distortions and illusions perpetuated by their fantasies. This process involves recognizing the difference between the idealized image they have created in their mind of the desired other and the actual person in reality (Willmott & Bentley, 2015). It requires acknowledging the imperfections and complexities of the desired other, as well as accepting the real-world limitations and uncertainties of the relationship.

Through CBT, individuals can develop healthier ways of thinking and behaving (Beck, 1991). By reframing cognitive biases, they can reduce the emotional intensity of limerent thoughts and cultivate a more balanced perspective of the desired person. For instance, individuals may examine how they overvalue fleeting moments of reciprocation or idealize qualities that may not even exist. Therapists can guide clients in building resilience and learning to manage obsessive thoughts through structured cognitive exercises.

Another important cognitive reframe for limerent individuals may involve addressing the scarcity mindset often present in limerence. Limerent individuals frequently believe there is only "one perfect person" who can fulfill their emotional needs. This belief may stem from early attachment wounds and the internalized fear that love and connection are limited or unpredictable. When something is perceived as rare or difficult to obtain, it becomes more desirable (Cialdini, 2021). The seeming unavailability of the desired other may amplify feelings of longing and attachment.

CBT may help clients reframe this scarcity mindset into one of abundance. By recognizing that there are countless opportunities for meaningful connections, individuals can reduce their fixation on a single person (Levine & Heller, 2012). Therapists can encourage clients to explore the variety of relationships and connections that bring richness to their lives, helping them move beyond the narrow laser focus of limerence.

Schema Therapy

Schema therapy is another intervention that may prove beneficial in the treatment of limerence. It focuses on identifying and changing deep-seated, maladaptive patterns or schemas that may underlie limerence and other emotional difficulties. By exploring the origins of these schemas and their impact on current functioning, individuals can work toward developing healthier ways of relating to themselves and others (Young et al., 2006).

One crucial aspect of schema therapy in the context of limerence may be reparenting the self. While direct healing with the parent who inflicted emotional neglect can sometimes be beneficial, this is not always possible or sufficient. Reparenting involves fostering an inner healthy adult who can meet the emotional needs that were unmet during childhood (Young et al., 2006). By nurturing this internal figure, individuals can cultivate a sense of security and self-worth that does not rely on external validation from the desired person.

Schema therapy may also address the role of early attachment wounds in limerence. Many limerent individuals experience a heightened sense of longing when someone is unavailable or reciprocation is ambiguous, which may stem from attachment wounds and a fear of scarcity in relationships (Willmott & Bentley, 2015). Using schema therapy, therapists can guide clients through the process recognizing how the limerence may be linked to early experiences of emotional neglect or unavailability, or even positive early childhood experiences they may be trying to emulate (Willmott & Bentley, 2015), and help them work toward a healthier relationship with themselves and others.

Attachment-Based Therapy

Since limerence involves intense and dysregulated attachment, attachment-based therapy may be a helpful intervention. This approach focuses on identifying and exploring the individual's attachment style, addressing unresolved attachment-related trauma, and supporting the development of more secure and balanced relational patterns (Wallin, 2015). In the context of limerence, therapists can guide individuals in understanding how early attachment experiences may be shaping their current emotional dependencies and idealizations. Over time, the therapeutic relationship itself may serve as a corrective emotional experience, helping to foster greater emotional regulation and more-secure internal models of connection.

Emotional Regulation

Emotional regulation techniques may be effective in managing the intense and fluctuating emotions associated with limerence. Developing these skills can support individuals in identifying, understanding, and modulating their emotional responses without resorting to compulsive behaviors or maladaptive coping strategies (Brach, 2013). Practices such as deep breathing, grounding exercises, and self-soothing techniques may provide relief during periods of emotional overwhelm and help individuals regain a sense of stability.

Behavioral Therapies

Behavioral therapies may be effective in treating limerence by identifying the behaviors that reinforce the fixation and replacing them with more-adaptive alternatives. Therapists can support clients in recognizing the rituals and compulsions associated with limerence and working to interrupt or eliminate them (Wyant, 2021).

This process may involve creating both physical and emotional distance from the desired other. Strategies include discontinuing all forms of communication, avoiding passive engagement on social media, and minimizing exposure to triggers that intensify limerent thoughts and emotional arousal.

Removing reminders such as messages, photos, or personal mementos linked to the desired person can also support detachment. In addition, avoiding locations or activities that reinforce the limerent narrative may help reduce emotional reactivity and make space for recovery. These behavioral adjustments contribute to an environment that supports emotional regulation and cognitive reframing.

Exposure Therapy

The central preoccupation in limerence is emotional reciprocation from the desired other. Conversely, the most feared experience is rejection or indifference. This intense fear sustains the obsessive and compulsive nature of limerent rumination. Consequently, exposure to imagined scenarios of rejection may help reduce the emotional reactivity that fuels limerence (Wyant, 2021).

One therapeutic strategy that may be effective is modifying the content of limerent fantasies. Instead of mentally rehearsing idealized scenarios of union or emotional closeness, individuals are encouraged to deliberately visualize scenarios in which the desired other rejects, dismisses, or shames them. Over time, repeated exposure to these imagined experiences may decrease the emotional charge associated with the fear of rejection, promoting greater emotional regulation and reducing compulsive thoughts. This approach mirrors imaginal exposure techniques used in the treatment of anxiety and trauma-related disorders.

Somatic Therapies

Somatic therapies emphasize the mind–body connection and may support individuals in processing the intense physiological arousal associated with limerence. Limerent states are frequently accompanied by physical sensations such as a racing heart, chest tightness, or a sense of emptiness (Willmott & Bentley, 2015). Approaches such as somatic experiencing, body scanning, or guided movement exercises can help individuals increase awareness of these sensations, regulate their nervous system, and release accumulated tension (van der Kolk, 2015).

By addressing the physiological dimension of limerence, somatic therapies may provide a holistic complement to cognitive, behavioral, and emotional interventions.

Psychoeducation

Psychoeducation plays a foundational role in treatment (Walsh, 2010). Educating clients about the nature of limerence can demystify their experience and reduce self-blame. When clients understand the neurobiological, psychological, and emotional factors driving their thoughts and behaviors, they may be better equipped to engage in therapeutic interventions. Providing information about the symptoms of limerence, the common trajectories of recovery, and the role of underlying causes may empower individuals to take an active role in their healing journey. Therapists may also include psychoeducation about healthy relationships, emotional regulation, and attachment dynamics, giving clients tools to foster deeper self-awareness.

Building a relapse prevention plan may involve the client creating action steps for managing urges, practicing mindfulness to stay grounded, and seeking support from trusted individuals or therapy groups. Helping clients anticipate challenges and proactively address them can fortify their resilience and prevent setbacks (Walsh, 2010). The LAS (see Appendix A) may also be introduced during psychoeducation to help individuals track symptom patterns over time and gain insight into the severity of their experience.

Group Therapy

Group therapy can provide a unique and supportive environment for individuals recovering from limerence. By sharing experiences with others who understand the intensity and challenges of limerence, participants can lean into a sense of community, reducing feelings of isolation. Group therapy offers a space to explore common themes, practice new coping strategies, and gain perspective from others' journeys (Fehr, 2018).

A structured, therapist-led group may also include exercises such as reframing narratives, practicing mindfulness, and exploring the role of attachment in limerence. These sessions may empower individuals to build resilience and lean into the collective journey of the group.

Grief Counseling

Grief counseling may also play a central role in recovery from limerence. It involves guiding individuals through key emotional tasks necessary to process and resolve grief (Worden, 2009). In the context of limerence, this process can support individuals in recognizing and accepting the loss associated with unrequited love or an unrealistic attachment. Specifically, it involves mourning the loss of the idealized bond and the hoped-for reciprocation from the desired person.

Therapists may find that, beneath the immediate grief surrounding the desired other, there may be deeper layers of unresolved grief linked to earlier experiences of loss, abandonment, or emotional deprivation. The intensity of limerence may reactivate these earlier wounds, bringing them into conscious awareness. Addressing this deeper grief can be an important step in healing the pain that underlies the limerent experience.

Through grief counseling, therapists can help clients process both the surface-level disappointment and the more foundational emotional losses from earlier life stages. This layered approach allows individuals to release the emotional hold of the limerent fixation and also grieve unaddressed earlier losses and begin to let go (Worden, 2009).

Narrative Therapy

Narrative therapy may also be beneficial in the treatment of limerence by offering an opportunity for individuals to explore and reshape the story of their limerence. This approach is based on the idea that people experience problems when the stories they or others have created about their lives do not align with their lived experiences (White & Epston, 1990). Limerence can feel like an all-encompassing epic, with themes of obsession, desire, and emotional dependency woven throughout its narrative (Willmott & Bentley, 2015). Narrative therapy may allow individuals to reclaim ownership of that story, shifting its trajectory from one of longing and stagnation to one of growth and transformation.

By working with a therapist, clients can safely examine the details of their story, exploring its emotional highs and lows, its themes of longing, and its perceived resolutions or lack thereof. The process of "re-storying" enables clients to reflect on these experiences in ways that support healing and change. Therapists guide individuals in identifying moments of agency within the narrative, reframing the story to highlight themes of growth, resilience, and authenticity (White & Epston, 1990).

For example, a limerent individual might feel trapped in a narrative of rejection and unfulfilled desire, where their identity is intertwined with the hope or despair associated with a romantic fixation. Through narrative therapy they can explore alternative perspectives, such as viewing their experience as a journey toward self-awareness or as an opportunity to uncover unmet emotional needs. This reframing may help clients see their limerence as a story they have the power to influence and shape.

Parts Work and Gestalt Therapy

Parts work and Gestalt therapy offer experiential approaches that help individuals explore the internal dynamics underlying limerence. Both modalities focus on increasing self-awareness, supporting internal integration, and giving voice to different aspects of the self that may be in conflict or seeking attention.

Parts work is based on the idea that the psyche is made up of various "parts" or subpersonalities, each with its own needs, fears, and beliefs. In the context of limerence, different parts of the individual may hold conflicting desires. For example, a longing part may cling to fantasies of union, while a protective part seeks to avoid rejection, and a critical part shames the individual for their perceived irrationality. These internal tensions can heighten distress and reinforce the compulsive cycle.

Therapeutic parts work invites individuals to explore these inner parts with curiosity and compassion. By dialoguing with the limerent part directly, individuals can begin to understand what the part is truly seeking. Rather than suppressing or rejecting this part, therapy encourages clients to listen, validate its experience, and support its integration into a more balanced internal system.

Gestalt therapy offers a complementary method of working with internal polarities through experiential techniques. One common approach is the "empty chair" exercise, where clients enact a dialogue between different parts of themselves. For example, a client might speak as the part that longs for connection, then respond from the part that feels ashamed or critical. Bringing these dynamics into the here and now can create emotional clarity, allowing individuals to process feelings that were previously unconscious or unresolved (Perls et al., 1951).

Depth Psychology: Dreamwork and Creative Therapies

Dreamwork and creative therapies can be profound tools for exploring the subconscious layers of limerence. Dreams may bring forth symbolic representations of unmet needs or unresolved conflicts. Jung emphasized that dreams are not random occurrences, but rather meaningful messages from the unconscious mind, offering insight into hidden desires, fears, and unresolved emotional experiences (Jung, 1995). Through guided dream analysis, individuals can uncover the deeper meanings behind their desires and attachments. For instance, a desired person may symbolize the anima or animus—the inner masculine or feminine archetype within the self—representing qualities that the dreamer unconsciously seeks to integrate. Recognizing this symbolic projection may allow individuals to reclaim these qualities within themselves, reducing their external dependency.

Creative outlets like journaling, art, or poetry may also allow individuals to externalize and process their emotions, providing an alternative medium to explore the complexities of limerence. Through these expressive forms, individuals can bring to light the deeper narratives shaping their emotional patterns. Working with these symbolic representations may help individuals shift their focus from the external desired person to the internal aspects of themselves that yearn for healing and integration. By engaging with symbols of their unconscious mind, individuals can uncover unaddressed emotional needs and develop healthier ways to fulfill them.

This approach transforms the longing into an opportunity for self-discovery and growth, as individuals gradually recognize that what they seek externally is usually an invitation to connect with their deeper self. By interpreting dreams, symbols, and creative expressions, individuals can begin to dismantle unhealthy attachments and cultivate a sense of wholeness rooted in internal integration.

Spirituality and Existential Therapy

Spirituality and existential therapy may offer a transformative lens through which individuals can reframe their longing. Rather than fixating on a single individual, this longing can be redirected as a yearning for divine union or a connection with the cosmos. Many spiritual traditions view longing not as a weakness but as a path to transcendence and unity with something greater than oneself. This approach involves leaning into the longing, not in pursuit of the external gratification of desire, but rather to explore the depth and meaning of the experience of yearning itself.

Existential therapy complements this reframing by addressing the existential dimensions of longing and connection. Existential therapy focuses on the individual's search for meaning, authenticity, and personal freedom (van Deurzen & Arnold-Baker, 2018). It recognizes that longing and existential angst are intrinsic to the human condition, arising from the tension between finite life and awareness of infinite possibilities beyond us. Therapists guide individuals to confront the realities of freedom, responsibility, and limitation, while also encouraging them to embrace longing as a portal for self-discovery and personal growth.

A defining feature of existential therapy is its recognition of the dynamic self and the paradoxical nature of human experience. Feelings of longing can be both painful and deeply meaningful. Therapists support clients in exploring this paradox, helping them shift focus from the external desired person to the internal aspects of self that are calling for attention, healing, and integration. Through a phenomenological attitude, clients are invited to engage directly with their lived experience without judgment and to understand longing as an expression of deeper existential yearnings, and a search for meaning, belonging, and wholeness.

From this perspective, yearning becomes a reflection of the universal human drive to connect with something larger than oneself. This reframing allows individuals to experience a sense of completeness that is not dependent on a particular person. The obsessive nature of limerence may be transformed into a sacred journey of personal growth, one that deepens understanding of the self and of one's place within a larger interconnected world. As van Deurzen and Arnold-Baker (2018) emphasize, the process of making meaning from life's challenges lies at the heart of existential therapy. It is through this meaning-making process that individuals can reimagine their longing as a catalyst for spiritual and psychological transformation.

Self-Care

Self-care and self-compassion may prove important components in the treatment of limerence. Encouraging individuals to prioritize their wellbeing, engage in meaningful activities, and respond to their struggles with kindness rather than self-criticism can create a strong foundation for recovery. According to Gobin (2019), self-care should be viewed as a holistic practice that addresses physical, emotional, spiritual, and social dimensions. This multifaceted approach allows individuals to attend to the underlying stressors and emotional patterns that contribute to limerence while developing healthier coping mechanisms and greater emotional resilience.

Cultivating self-compassion may be especially helpful in managing the setbacks and emotional turbulence of limerence. Rather than falling into cycles of shame or self-judgment, individuals are encouraged to relate to their pain with understanding and care. This gentler stance may support healing by reducing emotional reactivity and helping individuals maintain perspective during periods of heightened longing, ambiguity, or perceived rejection.

Practical self-care strategies might include journaling, mindful movement, time in nature, and creative or reflective practices, as well as caring properly for the physical body through good sleep and nutrition. These activities support emotional regulation and promote reconnection with the self. Over time, they may help individuals regain a sense of calm and inner stability.

Rebuilding and enriching one's life beyond the limerent focus is also essential. Pursuing personal goals, cultivating diverse relationships, and exploring new interests can expand sources of meaning and fulfillment. By redirecting attention from the desired other to personal growth, individuals begin to connect with a sense of identity that is not dependent on external validation.

This process may lead to a deeper, more grounded sense of self-worth rooted in personal values, not in the imagined reciprocation of a desired other. Self-care becomes not just a coping strategy, but a transformative practice that supports long-term healing and emotional wellbeing.

Pharmacological Interventions

Pharmacological interventions may present a potential avenue for the treatment of limerence, particularly due to its overlapping features with conditions such as depression, anxiety, addiction, and obsessive–compulsive disorder (Wakin & Vo, 2008; Willmott & Bentley, 2015; Wyant, 2021). While research in this area remains limited, the emotional intensity and compulsive thought patterns characteristic of limerence suggest that medications currently used for related conditions could offer relief. However, effective pharmacological strategies should be approached with caution and require further research.

Challenges to Treatment

The treatment of limerence may present several challenges, and individuals may encounter setbacks throughout the process.

One key obstacle is resistance to change. Limerence can become a deeply ingrained pattern of thought and emotion, making it difficult for individuals to release their attachment to the desired other. Even when it causes significant emotional distress, some people may hesitate to let go of the emotional intensity and euphoria it brings. Therapists may need to approach this gently, helping clients explore the potential benefits of moving beyond limerence and developing more-balanced emotional connections.

Another challenge is the fear of uncertainty. The desired other may symbolize safety, hope, or emotional fulfillment, and the idea of moving on can feel unsettling. Therapists can support clients in reframing this transition as a meaningful opportunity for growth, self-worth, and the possibility of more reciprocal and healthy relationships.

Relapse is also a possibility, as individuals may revert to patterns of obsessive thinking or behavior. These episodes, while difficult, can offer valuable insight into emotional triggers and highlight areas where coping strategies can be strengthened.

A further consideration is the risk of overreliance on the therapist. Some individuals may start to idealize their therapist or transfer attachment needs onto them. To manage this, therapists can hold compassionate boundaries while encouraging the client's autonomy through self-care, personal reflection, and connection with a broader support system.

Letting go of the desired other can evoke intense grief. Individuals may grieve not only the loss of the actual connection but also the fantasy they constructed around it. Therapists should provide a safe, nonjudgmental space for clients to process these complex emotions, and gently remind them that healing is rarely linear. Setbacks are not failures, but rather are part of the broader recovery journey.

The path to recovery from limerence is nuanced and highly individual. It requires a flexible, empathic approach that honors the complexity of each individual experience. While research is still emerging, current therapeutic models may offer some tools. By addressing psychological underpinnings, challenging unhelpful patterns, and engaging with the deeper emotional significance of longing, therapists can support individuals in moving beyond limerence and toward a more integrated, fulfilling life.

References

Beck, A. T. (1991). *Cognitive therapy and the emotional disorders*. Penguin Press.

Brach, T. (2013). *True refuge: Finding peace and freedom in your own awakened heart.* Bantam Dell Pub Group.

Cialdini, R. B. (2021). *Influence, new and expanded: The psychology of persuasion.* Harper Business.

Fehr, S. S. (2018). *Introduction to group therapy: A practical guide* (3rd ed.). Routledge.

Gobin, R. (2019). *The self-care prescription: Powerful solutions to manage stress, reduce anxiety & increase wellbeing.* Callisto Media.

Jung, C. G. (1995). *Memories, dreams, reflections* (New ed.). HarperCollins Publishers.

Levine, A., & Heller, R. (2012). *Attached: The new science of adult attachment and how it can help you find—and keep—love.* Jeremy P. Tarcher/Penguin.

Perls, F. S., Hefferline, R., & Goodman, P. (1951). *Gestalt therapy: Excitement and growth in the human personality* (Rev. ed.). Gestalt Journal Press.

van der Kolk, B. A. (2015). *The body keeps the score: Brain, mind, and body in the healing of trauma.* Penguin Books.

van Deurzen, E., & Arnold-Baker, C. (2018). *Existential therapy: Distinctive features.* Routledge.

Wakin, A. H., & Vo, D. B. (2008). Love-variant: The Wakin-Vo I.D.R. model of limerence. In Inter-Disciplinary.Net 2nd Global Conference: Challenging Intimate Boundaries. https://digitalcommons.sacredheart.edu/psych_fac/131/

Wallin, D. J. (2015). *Attachment in psychotherapy.* Guilford Press.

Walsh, J. (2010). *Psychoeducation in mental health.* Lyceum Books.

White, M., & Epston, D. (1990). *Narrative means to therapeutic ends.* W.W. Norton & Company.

Willmott, L., & Bentley, E. (2015). Exploring the lived-experience of limerence: A journey toward authenticity. *The Qualitative Report, 20*(1), 20–38. https://doi.org/10.46743/2160-3715/2015.1420

Worden, J. W. (2009). *Grief counselling and grief therapy: A handbook for the mental health practitioner* (4th ed.). Routledge.

Wyant, B. E. (2021). Treatment of limerence using a cognitive behavioral approach: A case study. *Journal of Patient Experience, 8,* 1–7. https://doi.org/10.1177/23743735211060812

Young, J. E., Klosko, J. S., & Weishaar, M. E. (2006). *Schema therapy: A practitioner's guide.* Guilford Press.

14 How Can I Help?

Supporting People with Limerence

Supporting someone experiencing limerence is a complex task, and doing so effectively requires guidance and understanding. Because limerence remains relatively unknown, most people are unfamiliar with what it is or how to respond to it in a supportive and informed way. Friends, family members, and partners may struggle to comprehend the depth of emotional distress that limerence causes, and their well-intentioned attempts to offer solutions, urge detachment, or minimize its significance can inadvertently worsen suffering for the individual. Witnessing someone locked in repetitive thought loops, analyzing minute interactions, and unable to disengage from their fixation can be exhausting and tiresome. Yet, true support does not come from dismissing or "fixing" the limerent individual but rather from deep patience, compassion, validation, and empathy. Through cultivating understanding rather than giving way to frustration, supporters can provide a space where healing is possible.

For individuals facing mental health challenges, recovery and management are rarely achieved in isolation. Communities, whether through family, friends, or broader social systems, play an essential role in creating the conditions for healing and in supporting long-term resilience. Those living with conditions such as anxiety or depression benefit from this collective understanding. Widespread awareness encourages empathy, access to care, and meaningful support. For individuals experiencing limerence, however, this support is lacking. The absence of societal recognition intensifies their suffering, leaving them to navigate the overwhelming emotional crisis of an involuntary and obsessive attachment while also confronting the isolation and misunderstanding that frequently accompany it.

Limerence remains largely invisible, creating a double burden for those who experience it. Individuals are consumed by intrusive thoughts, mood instability, and emotional dependency, while also facing the invalidation of their experiences. It is frequently misinterpreted as normal infatuation, poor self-control, or emotional weakness, which can lead to responses of confusion, frustration, or shame from those who might otherwise offer support. Without a proper framework for understanding, even well-meaning friends and family may unintentionally increase the limerent person's distress by offering misguided advice or minimizing their pain.

DOI: 10.4324/9781003563747-15

Raising awareness of limerence is an essential step in cultivating environments where support, management, and recovery can take place. Community education can reduce stigma, promote informed care, and help individuals manage the condition while also addressing the isolation and shame that arise from being misunderstood. Recognizing and addressing this gap is crucial to ensuring that those experiencing limerence receive the understanding and support needed to regain emotional stability and wellbeing.

Active Listening and Validation

One crucial aspect of supporting someone experiencing limerence is active listening, the practice of offering one's full attention without judgment or the intent to immediately offer solutions. Limerent individuals often feel isolated in their experience, particularly because the nature of limerence can seem irrational or excessive to those who have not experienced it firsthand. As a result, they may be hesitant to share their feelings, fearing that they will be dismissed, mocked, or misunderstood. When a trusted friend or family member listens with genuine interest, maintains eye contact, and reflects back what they hear, it provides a powerful counterbalance to the shame and self-doubt that the individual may have internalized. Simple affirmations such as "That sounds really overwhelming" or "I can see why this is so consuming for you" can be profoundly reassuring, signaling to the individual that their experiences are being acknowledged rather than dismissed.

It is equally important to avoid invalidating responses, such as urging the individual to "just move on" or suggesting that their emotions are exaggerated. While such statements may stem from a well-intentioned desire to encourage emotional resilience, they usually have the opposite effect, reinforcing the individual's sense of isolation. Instead, effective support involves meeting the limerent individual where they are emotionally, allowing them to articulate their feelings without pressure to change or suppress them. Paradoxically, it is this very process of being heard and accepted that can facilitate emotional flexibility and change. Demonstrating consistent and nonjudgmental support can help the limerent individual feel safe enough to explore their emotions more deeply and work toward a greater sense of emotional freedom.

It is crucial not to judge or shame a limerent individual for their experience. Limerence is an involuntary state that a person has very little control over, and criticism or moralizing will only deepen their distress. Labeling limerence as immature or impulsive is particularly damaging, as it disregards the suffering of the individual and the depth of their internal experience. Instead, offering a nonjudgmental space where they feel safe to express themselves can provide relief from the isolation that accompanies the experience.

Additionally, when limerent individuals become fixated on details of interactions with the desired other, searching for signs of reciprocation or rejection, dismissing them outright as "delusional" or "irrational" can be profoundly damaging. Instead, a validating response such as, "I can see why that moment stood out to you" acknowledges their experience without reinforcing obsessive thought loops. The goal is not to feed the fixation but to offer a reality-grounded space where they feel understood rather than shamed or criticized.

Responding to a Limerent Confession

When someone experiencing limerence expresses their feelings to the desired other, that person may feel caught off guard or unsure of how to respond. Whether they are aware of the intensity of the limerent feelings or not, the best way for the desired other to handle the situation is with honesty, clarity, and kindness. If the feelings are not mutual, the most compassionate approach is to be direct while remaining sensitive. Avoiding a definitive response or leaving room for ambiguity is harmful, as limerent individuals cling to any perceived hope, which ultimately prolongs emotional distress. Even a vague or neutral response can inadvertently sustain obsessive fixation.

A clear and respectful response such as, "I really appreciate your honesty, but I don't share the same feelings," provides closure while acknowledging their courage in expressing themselves. The worst thing to do is to give mixed signals, delay a response, or offer false hope, as this will intensify their emotional turmoil. While it may feel difficult to be so direct, ambiguity only exacerbates suffering. By offering clarity, the desired person helps the limerent individual begin the process of moving forward, rather than remaining stuck in a cycle of longing and uncertainty.

Additionally, being compassionate in response to their vulnerability is key. Acknowledging their emotions and reassuring them that their feelings are valid, even if unreciprocated, can prevent them from feeling ashamed or foolish. Statements like, "I understand this must have been difficult to share," or "I respect and appreciate you, even if I don't feel the same way romantically," can soften the impact while maintaining honesty. By handling the situation with directness and care, the desired person can offer the limerent individual the relief of certainty and the opportunity to heal.

Partners of Limerent Individuals

For partners of individuals experiencing limerence for someone else, the emotional toll can be significant. Discovering that one's partner is caught in obsessive thoughts and intense longing for another person can evoke feelings of rejection, insecurity, and deep hurt. It is important to understand, however, that while individuals should be held accountable for their actions, limerence is an involuntary psychological state rather than a deliberate betrayal. When a limerent individual feels safe enough to be open about their experience, they are more likely to continue sharing rather than withdrawing into secrecy. This honesty can preserve trust and create a space where both partners can navigate the situation together, rather than allowing it to become a source of division.

While responding with compassion is essential, the partner of a limerent individual must also honor their own emotional needs and boundaries. Supporting a partner through limerence does not mean suppressing personal feelings or compromising wellbeing. It is natural to experience pain, frustration, or resentment, and these emotions are valid. The key is to approach the situation with both empathy and self-respect. Partners should feel empowered to set clear and loving boundaries that protect against emotional exhaustion or the development of codependent patterns.

Creating an open space where both individuals can share their emotions without fear of judgment encourages deeper understanding. Recognizing that limerence reflects an internal emotional experience rather than dissatisfaction with the relationship can help prevent misplaced blame or self-doubt. Couples therapy with a clinician who understands limerence can provide vital support, offering tools to process difficult emotions, improve communication, and strengthen the connection between partners.

Maintaining clear boundaries is especially important. For instance, if the limerent individual frequently talks about the desired other in ways that feel distressing, their partner has every right to respond with care and clarity, such as by saying, "I want to support you, but I also need to protect my own emotional space. Let's find another way to help you process this." With mutual understanding, patience, and ongoing dialogue, it is possible for couples to move through this experience with a deeper foundation of honesty and emotional resilience.

Ethical and Moral Complexities

Limerence is not always straightforward. Sometimes, it manifests in situations that bring moral and ethical dilemmas, such as when a person is limerent for someone who is in a committed relationship, in a position of authority, or when the limerent individual is already in a committed, monogamous relationship. These situations can create intense internal conflict, as the limerent individual may feel guilt, shame, or confusion about their emotions. A compassionate and ethical approach acknowledges two truths simultaneously: limerence is involuntary and not a choice, but actions remain a choice. While experiencing limerence is not inherently immoral, how the limerent individual responds to it carries ethical weight.

Throwing morality in someone's face or socially ostracizing them for their involuntary obsession, however, is cruel and counterproductive. Helping them navigate their emotions ethically and responsibly is a far more constructive and supportive approach. Instead of moralizing, guiding the limerent individual toward introspection is more effective. Encouraging them to reflect on what the desired other represents and what underlying emotional needs might be at play can shift the focus inward. Supporting them in establishing clear personal and external boundaries helps them act in alignment with their values. If the limerent individual is overwhelmed with guilt, it is important to remind them that having unwanted thoughts and feelings does not make them a bad person. Self-compassion allows for greater clarity and better decision-making.

Emotional Wellbeing of Support People

Supporting a limerent individual can be emotionally taxing. Friends, family, and partners may find themselves in the role of an emotional anchor, absorbing distress, listening to repeated analyses of the same situation, and trying to be patient as the limerent individual works through obsessive thoughts and compulsive loops. Without self-awareness and boundaries, this can lead to compassion fatigue and emotional burnout.

It is essential that support people regularly check in with their own emotional wellbeing and practice self-care. Recognizing personal limits, seeking support from other trusted friends, and encouraging the limerent individual to seek professional help can prevent their overreliance on one person or group. It is not selfish for supporters to prioritize their own mental health. Setting emotional boundaries and taking time for self-care ensures that support remains sustainable.

Not everyone is suited to this role, and acknowledging that is crucial. To effectively support a limerent individual, one must possess patience, compassion, emotional strength, and a genuine concern for the person's wellbeing. Without these qualities, support may become ineffective or even detrimental, reinforcing patterns of distress rather than alleviating them. Those offering support must assess their willingness, capacity, and emotional resources, recognizing that limerence can persist for months, years, or even decades, and that sustained support requires endurance.

The most effective support comes from those who do not turn away in frustration, shame, or judgment but instead meet the limerent individual where they are, patiently engaging with their consistent longing and obsessive thoughts before gently guiding them back to themselves and to reality. They offer a steady presence, providing a much-needed dose of perspective without cruelty or condescension. Unlike those who dismiss, moralize, or ostracize, they recognize that true support is not about rejection or condemnation, but rather about helping the limerent individual find their way back to clarity with their dignity and self-esteem intact.

Conclusion

Where Do We Go from Here?

This book has sought to unravel the intricate web of limerence, to illuminate its causes, consequences, and complexities. From its neurobiological under-pinnings to its cultural manifestations, limerence is not just an individual afflic-tion but one that impacts shared human experience. Understanding it is the first step toward liberation and insight.

At its core, limerence is a deep longing for connection, a hunger for some-thing that feels absent, just beyond reach. Beneath the symptoms, neuroses, and pathology lies a yearning: an insatiable desire for nourishment, comfort, union, fulfillment, completeness, or *manna*, the symbol of divine sustenance. The longing itself is not the sickness. The need to love and be loved is not patho-logical: It is a fundamental and defining feature of human existence. What renders limerence destructive is the entanglement of this yearning with fear, absence, obsession, and pain. It is the dysfunction of unmet needs, unresolved attachment wounds, and an imbalanced state of mind that twists this hunger into something that devours rather than nourishes.

Limerence is not love, but it is born of the same fire. It is a distortion of the longing for love, tangled in fixation, obsession, and a desperate, looping search for emotional reciprocation. Those without a healthy blueprint for love and connection, who have only known emotional inconsistency or deprivation, may be particularly vulnerable. Limerence is a repeated grasping at substitutes, constructing fantasies of fulfillment around a desired other, projecting all that is missing onto a single external figure.

Limerence is a thief of time, stealing moments of a person's life, hijacking the present, redirecting thought and energy again and again toward the unreal or unattainable. It is the antithesis of presence, of mindfulness, of gratitude. It is the antithesis of mental stability, robbing an individual of peace of mind in each moment.

Limerence reveals the human desire for fulfillment, and also the sense of its unattainability. It is the hunger of the self, seeking wholeness in the external, and that, when left unchecked, leads to compulsion, addiction, and profound suffering. If limerence is a signal, then it conveys impor-tant psychological insights. It may indicate unresolved emotional wounds,

DOI: 10.4324/9781003563747-16

unmet attachment needs, and repressed parts of the self that seek recognition. Understanding limerence as a signal allows for a shift in perspective. Instead of merely resisting its grip, those affected can use limerence as a guide toward greater self-awareness and integration. Examining the underlying psychological structures that contribute to limerence can help individuals gain insight into their emotional responses and relational patterns.

Recovery from limerence is not about extinguishing the ability to love intensely, but about learning to love in a way that is free rather than frantic, and expansive rather than entrapping. Healing begins when the individual recognizes that limerence is not love, but rather a craving for love distorted by pain, fear, and obsession. The process of healing involves reclaiming the capacity for genuine connection, building self-worth that is not contingent on external validation, and cultivating relationships based on reciprocity rather than fantasy and obsession.

Despite the profound impact limerence has on mental and emotional well-being, it remains an under-researched phenomenon. It sits at the intersection of multiple disciplines, including neuroscience, psychology, psychiatry, and sociology. No single field has fully taken ownership of studying its mechanisms and consequences. Advancing research in this area is essential for improving clinical interventions and broadening scientific understanding. To achieve this, greater collaboration between disciplines is needed. Integrating perspectives from neuroscience, psychology, psychiatry, and sociology can create a more comprehensive framework that reflects the biological, psychological, and cultural dimensions of limerence.

One crucial step in this endeavor may be mapping the neurobiological basis of limerence. Neuroimaging studies using techniques such as positron emission tomography (PET) and functional magnetic resonance imaging (fMRI) could provide insight into the neural circuits involved in limerence. If research confirms that limerence has a unique pattern or operates similarly to addiction or obsessive–compulsive disorder at a neurobiological level, this could inform the development of pharmacological and psychotherapeutic interventions.

Additionally, research must examine the role of the limbic system, particularly the amygdala and anterior cingulate cortex, in processing the emotional highs and lows associated with limerence. If hyperactivity in these regions correlates with intrusive thoughts and emotional dysregulation, therapeutic interventions could be designed to modulate these neural patterns. The more that is understood about the neurological underpinnings of limerence, the better equipped clinicians will be to offer targeted, evidence-based treatments.

Beyond neurobiology, psychological research must investigate the developmental pathways that contribute to limerence. Longitudinal studies tracking individuals from childhood to adulthood could provide valuable insights into how early attachment disruptions may shape susceptibility to limerence. Understanding these developmental trajectories can inform early intervention strategies.

Additionally, cultural expectations and social conditioning may shape how limerence manifests. Gender roles may influence how individuals express or repress limerent emotions, while societal norms may dictate whether limerence is romanticized, pathologized, or dismissed altogether. Understanding these sociocultural influences is crucial for developing nuanced, inclusive interventions.

Clinical psychology must establish precise screening mechanisms to identify individuals at risk of limerence. Many people who suffer from limerence do not recognize their experience as distinct from ordinary romantic attraction, and may only seek professional help once their condition has reached a critical level of distress. The Limerence Assessment Scale introduced in this book, along with a proposed DSM-style diagnostic framework and clinical decision-making guide, are steps toward that aim. Validated tools of this kind would enable clinicians to intervene earlier, offer targeted support, and reduce long-term psychological distress.

The study of limerence is still in its early stages. It is imperative that researchers, clinicians, and mental health experts recognize the widespread impact of limerence and take decisive steps toward formalizing diagnostic criteria, expanding treatment modalities, and integrating limerence into broader discussions of mental health. Without dedicated attention, individuals struggling with limerence will continue to suffer in silence, lacking the support and recognition necessary for recovery. While the phenomenon has been observed and described for decades, significant gaps remain in understanding its origins, its neurological basis, and its long-term psychological consequences.

So, where do we go from here? We must begin by taking limerence seriously, both to better support those who suffer from it and to deepen our understanding of the processing it involves. By researching this condition with greater urgency, we can uncover insights into human attachment, emotional healing, and the psychological patterns that shape our inner world.

To pathologize limerence is not to reduce it to a disorder alone. Just as depression can lead to existential growth, and anxiety can enhance connection with self, limerence also holds the potential to transform. It is a condition that causes distress, but it also reveals emotional truths that, if explored, can guide deep healing through psychic integration.

Understanding limerence demands that we look inward and ask what it reveals about the nature of longing itself. By grounding limerence in science while honoring its existential and symbolic dimensions, a more integrated model of care becomes possible. This model recognizes the pathological elements of limerence, such as obsessive preoccupation, emotional dependency, and compulsive behaviors, while still holding space for the deeper psychological and spiritual potential it holds.

In many traditions, the longing for union with another mirrors the soul's yearning for divine connection. Recognizing this broader dimension of longing may open new avenues for healing through practices that cultivate self-awareness, presence, and spiritual fulfillment. It requires a shift from seeking completion in another to finding it within. It is essential to distinguish between limerence and love, encouraging relationships that are based on mutual respect, reciprocity, and genuine emotional connection.

Limerence is a distressing, involuntary psychological condition. Yet it also reflects the profound capacity of the human mind to form emotional bonds, engage in imaginative projection, and experience deep longing. It is not merely a dysfunction to be eradicated, but a phenomenon to be explored, supported, and understood.

By approaching limerence with scientific curiosity and compassionate inquiry, we can ease distress for those suffering in silence while simultaneously illuminating one of the deepest and most compelling mysteries of the human experience. In tracing the intricate contours of obsessive love, we may begin to understand the mechanisms of desire and the ancient architecture of longing itself. We catch glimpses of our restless pursuit for meaning, for wholeness, and for the elusive promise of connection and fulfillment, a yearning intricately woven into our collective humanity.

In recognizing limerence as both affliction and revelation, we confront the delicate balance between loving deeply and loving pathologically. To love intensely is healthy and human, yet to love obsessively is surrendering emotional freedom to an illusion, a seductive promise that distorts perception and erodes the very sense of union it claims to offer.

Limerence is the altar of love's madness, the threshold where love becomes obsession. It begins as a projection cast onto the external other, but when we trace it back to its source we find that it is, in fact, a mirror in which the deepest, oldest, and most hidden parts of the self are reflected and made visible. The process is disorienting, destabilizing, and painful, but with the right tools and the right guide, limerence may become a powerful gateway for transformation and healing.

Appendices

Appendix A
Limerence Assessment Scale (LAS)

The following appendices provide the structured resources and tools referenced throughout this book. These include assessment scales and clinical materials intended to support diagnosis, formulation, and treatment planning in both therapeutic and research settings. Each appendix is designed to be used flexibly and adapted as needed for individual contexts.

The Limerence Assessment Scale (LAS) is a self-report screening tool designed to help identify the presence and severity of limerence. It was developed in response to the absence of validated clinical instruments addressing this experience and aims to support both clinicians and individuals in recognizing the emotional, cognitive, and behavioral patterns that may indicate pathological limerence.

The scale includes 15 items grouped into four domains: intrusive thoughts, compulsive behaviors, emotional dependency, and functional impairment. While the LAS has not yet undergone formal psychometric validation, it offers a structured starting point for assessment and clinical discussion.

Instructions

Please reflect on your experience over the past four weeks and rate how frequently you have experienced each of the following thoughts, feelings, or behaviors in relation to a specific person (the desired other).

Rating scale:

- 0 = Not at all
- 1 = Rarely
- 2 = Sometimes
- 3 = Frequently
- 4 = Almost constantly

Section A: Intrusive Thoughts and Preoccupation

1 I think about this person even when I try not to.
2 My thoughts about this person interrupt my ability to focus on work, study, or everyday tasks.
3 I replay past interactions with this person over and over in my mind.

4 I fantasize about future interactions or conversations with this person.
5 I wonder obsessively about what this person thinks or feels about me.

Section B: Compulsive Behaviors

6 I check this person's social media or online activity more often than I want to.
7 I reread old messages or revisit past interactions with this person repeatedly.
8 I analyze or interpret small details of their behavior or communication to find signs of reciprocation.

Section C: Emotional Dependency

9 My mood changes dramatically based on whether I feel this person is responding to me positively or not.
10 I feel emotionally dependent on signs of affection, approval, or attention from this person.
11 I find it very difficult to emotionally detach, even when I know the connection is unlikely or unavailable.
12 I focus mostly on this person's positive traits and overlook flaws or incompatibilities.

Section D: Functional Impairment

13 My thoughts or preoccupation with this person interfere with my ability to engage fully in other important relationships.
14 I avoid certain places, people, or activities because of my emotional reaction to this person.
15 I experience changes in sleep, appetite, mood, concentration, or other aspects of wellbeing because of this experience.

Scoring

Add the scores for all 15 items.
  Total possible score: 60
  Score interpretation:

- 0–14: Subclinical or normative
- 15–29: Mild symptoms; psychoeducation may be sufficient
- 30–44: Moderate symptoms; clinical intervention is advisable
- 45–60: Severe symptoms; diagnostic criteria for Limerence Disorder may be met

Note

The LAS is intended for therapeutic, educational, or exploratory purposes and is not a substitute for formal diagnosis. Interpretation should occur within a broader clinical context, incorporating case formulation and individual history. High scores should prompt further exploration rather than definitive conclusions.

Appendix B
Clinical Decision-Making Guide— Working with Limerence

This clinical guide is intended to help therapists assess and conceptualize limerence in clients presenting with obsessive romantic thoughts, emotional dependency, or fixation on a desired other. It offers a step-by-step framework for determining whether the client's experience may reflect limerence disorder, and how to proceed with treatment or referral.

Step 1: Establish Clinical Relevance

Ask the client:

- How long have you felt this way about this person?
- How much is it affecting your work, relationships, sleep, or wellbeing?
- Have you tried to stop thinking about them, and what happened when you tried?
- Do you feel emotionally dependent on their attention, approval, or contact?

Proceed to Step 2 if the preoccupation has lasted at least three months and significantly impairs functioning.

Step 2: Rule Out Alternative Diagnoses

Use clinical judgment to consider whether the experience may be better explained by:

- obsessive–compulsive disorder (e.g. obsessions unrelated to interpersonal longing)
- bipolar disorder (e.g. affective instability across contexts, not tied to one person)
- attachment-related trauma or generalized dependency (across multiple relationships)
- delusional disorder (e.g. erotomania without insight or reality testing)

If none of these fully account for the symptoms, proceed to Step 3.

Step 3: Assess for Limerence Features

Does the client report:

- intrusive, unwanted thoughts about the desired other
- emotional volatility in response to perceived attention or rejection
- recurrent checking, ruminating, fantasizing, or analyzing of interactions
- difficulty functioning or disengaging despite insight or attempts to stop

If yes to most, complete the Limerence Assessment Scale (Appendix A) and consider a working formulation of limerence disorder.

Step 4: Tailor the Treatment Approach

Depending on the client's presentation, consider the following strategies:

- **Psychoeducation**: Normalize the intensity while validating the distress.
- **Cognitive behavioral techniques**: These include thought tracking, behavioral experiments, response prevention.
- **Emotional regulation**: Build skills to tolerate distress and uncertainty without compulsive action.
- **Attachment work**: Explore early patterns that may be activated in the current experience.
- **Narrative or imagery interventions**: Separate fantasy from reality, and strengthen identity outside the limerent focus.
- **Relapse planning**: Prepare for potential future limerent episodes or transferences.

Therapeutic approaches may need to be flexible, especially when symptoms overlap with anxiety, trauma, or unresolved grief.

Clinical Note

Some clients are ambivalent about losing their limerence due to its perceived intensity, beauty, or connection to creativity or hope. Work with ambivalence compassionately. Emphasize that healing does not mean emotional numbing, but rather regaining autonomy and clarity.

Appendix C
Client Reflection Prompts—Understanding and Working Through Limerence

The following journaling prompts are intended to support individuals experiencing limerence. These questions are designed to help bring unconscious patterns into conscious awareness, challenge cognitive distortions, and explore the emotional and relational significance of the desired other.

Clients may use these prompts in a personal journal or share responses with their therapist as part of ongoing treatment.

Section 1: Understanding the Experience

1 When did I first notice I was thinking about this person more than usual? What was happening in my life at the time?
2 What do I believe I need from this person that feels unavailable elsewhere?
3 What emotions come up most strongly when I think about them (e.g. hope, fear, shame, joy)?
4 What is the fantasy version of this person or relationship? How does that compare to what I know or have experienced with them?
5 If I could receive exactly what I want from them right now, what would that be, and what would it mean to me?

Section 2: Challenging the Cycle

6 What do I do (mentally or behaviorally) to keep the fantasy or connection alive? How does that affect my mood?
7 Have I tried to reduce my contact, thoughts, or focus on them before? What helped or got in the way?
8 In what ways has this fixation impacted my work, relationships, self-esteem, or emotional wellbeing?
9 What would it mean to begin letting go, even a little? What part of me might resist that?
10 What do I fear might happen if I stop thinking about them or hoping for reciprocation?

Section 3: Reclaiming Self and Identity

11 What are three things I value about myself that have nothing to do with this person?
12 Who or what in my life has offered me connection or safety in the past?
13 What are the unmet emotional needs I might be projecting onto this person?
14 How can I begin to meet some of those needs within myself, or with others in healthier ways?
15 What does healing from this experience look like for me—not just symptom relief, but actual growth?

Suggested Use

These prompts are best used over time, with space for reflection and emotional integration. Clients may benefit from revisiting certain questions as their insight deepens. Therapists can also select specific prompts based on clinical goals or session themes.

Index

Note: *Italic* page numbers refer to figures.

GAD *see* generalized anxiety disorder (GAD)
gender: differences 86–87; and digital limerence 108
generalized anxiety disorder (GAD) 3, 4
Gestalt therapy 129
Gobin, R. 131
golden apple, the 29–30
grief counseling 128
group therapy 127–128
Guicciardi, J. "Giulietta" 96

Harvest (Young) 96
Holiday: *Don't Explain* 97
human longing 45–47
hungry ghost 47

idealized fantasy 62–63
incubation 61
infatuation 1, 6, 7, 26, 27, 56, 62, 89, 92, 94, 97, 99, 103, 112, 117–119, 134
insecure attachment 16, 18, 20, 87
intermittent reinforcement 50–51, 104
intrusive thinking 54
intrusive thoughts 4, 6, 7, 33, 37, 54, 55, 68, 82, 86, 103, 111, 112, 114, 116, 117, 124, 134, 140, 143–144
I Put a Spell on You (Simone) 97
ironic processes, theory of 58
Isaak, C.: *Wicked Game* 97
ishq 45
I've Come Again (Rumi) 93

Jung, C. 22, 30, 31, 33

Kabbalistic thought 44
kama 44

LAS *see* Limerence Assessment Scale (LAS)
Lévy, H.-L.: *Young Woman and Death* 89–90, *91*
Light as a Breeze (Cohen) 96
Lilac Wine (Simone) 97
limerence 6–9; anxious attachment and 18–19; archetypes of 22–33; avoidant attachment and 19; challenges to treatment 132–133; characteristics of 18; definition of 1; and differentiation from healthy love 1; digital 102–109;

disorder 118, 119, 147–148; legacy of 100; as maladaptive coping mechanism 19–20; mutual 68–71; neurochemistry of 35–42; pathological nature of 111–113; progression of 1; proposed diagnostic criteria 118–119; unexpressed 71–75; unrequited 75–77; *see also individual entries*
Limerence Assessment Scale (LAS) 113, 119–120, 123, 127, 141, 145–146
limerent confession, responding to 136
limerent dreams 58–59
limerent fantasy 61–62; dysfunction of 66–67; functions of 66; impacts of 64–66; themes of 63–64
limerent thoughts 55–56
Linehan, M. 3
literature 92–95
longing 6, 8, 28, 33, 44–51, 56, 57, 62, 65–68, 70, 71, 75, 77, 81, 83, 84–86, 89–100, 102, 103, 112, 124, 125, 128–131, 133, 138, 139, 141, 142; divine 44, 45, 94; emotional 63; human 45–47; intense 1, 7, 18, 21, 64, 94, 115, 117, 136; interpersonal 147; irrational 32; misdirected 47–48; obsessive 80, 96, 99, 100, 114; profound 23, 25, 26, 44, 97; for reciprocation 49–50, 72; romantic 22, 98, 116; unhealed 27
love 5–6, 11–21; bond 6; erotic 22; romantic 6, 23, 28, 35–37, 84, 98, 102, 114, 115, 120
Love Actually (2003) 99
Lover, You Should've Come Over (Buckley) 97
Love Sick (Dylan) 96

major depressive disorder 4, 117
Make You Feel My Love (Dylan) 96
maladaptive developmental attachment 16–21
Millais, J. E.: *Ophelia* 90, *92*
Miller, H. 94–95
mindfulness-based intervention 46, 74, 124, 139
mind-wandering 60, 61
Minogue, K.: *Can't Get You Out of My Head* 97

For Product Safety Concerns and Information please contact our EU
representative GPSR@taylorandfrancis.com
Taylor & Francis Verlag GmbH, Kaufingerstraße 24, 80331 München, Germany

www.ingramcontent.com/pod-product-compliance
Lightning Source LLC
Chambersburg PA
CBHW052010270326
41929CB00015B/2858